BEST

NONFICTION

Middle Level

7 Selections for Young People

with Lessons for Teaching the Basic Elements of Nonfiction

Christine Lind Orciuch
Theodore Knight, Ph. D.

JAMESTOWN PUBLISHERS

a division of NTC/CONTEMPORARY PUBLISHING GROUP
Lincolnwood, Illinois USA

Cover Design: Steve Straus   **Cover Illustration:** Lori Lohstoeter
Interior Design: Steve Straus

Interior Illustrations
Unit 1: Corbis-Bettmann
Unit 2: Artist, Jan Matzeliger: Lois Mailoudones, © the Associated Publishers
Photo of Elijah McCoy: Moorland-Springarn Research Center,
   Howard University (page 30)
Unit 3: © Bill Wassman/The Stock Market (page 56)
Unit 4: Culver Pictures (page 92)
Unit 5: © Randy Ury/The Stock Market (page 130)
Unit 6: © A. Ramey/Woodfin Camp & Associates (page 160)
Unit 7: © Charles Krebs/The Stock Market (page 192)

ISBN: 0-89061-899-2 (hardbound)
ISBN: 0-89061-883-6 (softbound)

Published by Jamestown Publishers,
a division of NTC/Contemporary Publishing Group, Inc.
4255 West Touhy Avenue
Lincolnwood (Chicago), Illinois 60646-1975, U.S.A.
© 1998 NTC/Contemporary Publishing Group, Inc.

890 QB 0987654321

ACKNOWLEDGMENTS

Acknowledgment is gratefully made to the following publishers, authors, and agents for permission to reprint these works. Every effort has been made to determine copyright owners. In the case of any omissions, the Publisher will be pleased to make suitable acknowledgments in future editions.

"The Icing of the Cream" by Becky Rupp. First published in the August 1986 issue of *Country Journal*. Reprinted by permission of the author. All rights reserved.

"Jan Matzeliger and 'The Real McCoy' " by Jim Haskins from *Outward Dreams, Black Inventors and Their Inventions*. Copyright © 1992 by Jim Haskins. Reprinted with permission from Walker and Company, 435 Hudson Street, New York, New York, 10014. All rights reserved.

"Pompeii: A Snapshot in Time" excerpts from "Pompeii" from *Lost Cities and Vanished Civilizations* by Robert Silverberg. A Bantam Book, published by arrangement with the Chilton Company. Copyright © 1962 by Robert Silverberg. Published by permission of Agberg, Ltd., c/o Ralph M. Vicinanza, Ltd.

"The Soul Selects Her Own Society" from *I'm Nobody, Who Are You?* by Edna Barth. Text copyright © 1971 by Edna Barth. Reprinted by permission of Clarion Books/Houghton Mifflin Company. All rights reserved.

"Friendship" from *I Know Why the Caged Bird Sings* by Maya Angelou. Copyright © 1969 by Maya Angelou. Reprinted by permission of Random House, Inc.

"Sin Papeles" from *The Uncertain Journey* by Margaret Poynter. Reprinted with the permission of Atheneum Books for Young Readers, an imprint of Simon & Schuster Children's Publishing Division. Copyright © 1992 Margaret Poynter.

"A Good Deed Goes Wrong" from *Real Ponies Don't Go Oink!* by Patrick McManus, © 1974 by Patrick McManus. Reprinted by permission of Henry Holt and Company, Inc.

CONTENTS

TO THE STUDENT

Nonfiction is literature about real people, places, and events—unlike fiction, which comes mostly from a writer's imagination. When you read magazine or newspaper articles, history books, instructional manuals or guides, biographies and autobiographies, and diaries or journals, you are reading nonfiction. The life story of Martin Luther King, Jr., a science article about the latest research into heart disease, or a cookbook about desserts are other examples of nonfiction. To many people, good nonfiction is as interesting as, or even more interesting than, fiction.

Writers of nonfiction examine real people, events, and experiences in order to understand them. Like all writers, nonfiction writers try to communicate their thoughts, feelings, and ideas about a subject. They may want to explain why certain events happened, to describe an interesting person, place, or incident, or to persuade you to follow a particular course of action. An author's purpose in writing shapes his or her work.

People read nonfiction to gain understanding. They may be curious about a subject—the person, event, or idea—that the writer has chosen to write about. To keep the interest of their readers, writers must not only organize the information but also choose what facts to include and emphasize. In this book you will learn skills that will help you analyze how writers develop and organize their material to create lively, interesting works of nonfiction. By understanding how good writers communicate and by studying the works of good nonfiction writers, you can learn techniques to improve your own writing.

Each unit in this book contains a nonfiction selection and lessons that teach concepts and skills that will help you interpret the selection and help you understand the particular techniques the author uses to accomplish his or her purpose. Each unit also includes writing exercises that provide an opportunity to use what you learn in the lessons in your own writing.

UNIT FORMAT AND ACTIVITIES

- Each unit begins with a photograph or an illustration depicting someone or something connected with the selection. The photograph or illustration will help you make some predictions about the selection.

- The Introduction begins with background information about the selection and its author. Important literary concepts and skills are then presented, and you are given an opportunity to begin developing these concepts and skills in your own writing. Finally, there are questions for you to consider as you read. These questions will help you focus on the concepts and skills presented in the unit's lessons.

- The selection makes up the next section. It may be a complete work, such as an essay or an article, or an excerpt from a biography, autobiography, or diary.

- Following each selection are questions that test your comprehension of the events and other elements of the selection as well as your critical thinking skills. Your answers to these questions and to other exercises in the unit should be recorded in a personal literature notebook. Check your answers with your teacher.

- Your teacher may provide you with charts to record your progress in developing your comprehension skills: The Comprehension Skills Graph *records* your scores and the Comprehension Skills Profile *analyzes* your scores—providing you with information about the skills on which you need to focus. You can talk with your teacher about ways to work on those comprehension skills.

- The next section begins with a discussion of the literary concept that is the unit's focus. The discussion is followed by three lessons, each of which illustrates a technique the author uses to develop that concept. For example, you will see how an author of a persuasive essay expresses opinions, supports those opinions, and uses loaded language to persuade her audience to understand and accept her motives and actions.

- Short-answer exercises test your understanding of the author's techniques as illustrated by short excerpts from the selection. You can check your answers to the exercises with your teacher and determine what you need to review.
- Each lesson also includes a writing exercise that guides you in creating your own original nonfiction work using the techniques you have just studied.
- Discussion guides and a final writing activity round out each unit in the book. These activities will help sharpen your reading, thinking, speaking, and writing skills.

Reading the selections in this book will enable you to recognize and appreciate the skills it takes to write interesting nonfiction. When you understand what makes good nonfiction, you become a better reader. The writing exercises and assignments will help you become a better writer by giving you practice in using the authors' techniques to make your own nonfiction writing interesting.

Author's Purpose

Buying a Peerless Freezer
WITH THE
Vacuum Screw Dasher.

The Icing of the Cream

by Becky Rupp

INTRODUCTION

BUILDING
BACKGROUND

Almost everyone loves ice cream. It is one of the most popular desserts in the United States. It is so popular, in fact, that many people have made their fortunes from it. Just think of names such as Howard Johnson and Ben and Jerry. If you are used to buying ice cream in a store, you may wonder why anyone would want to know how to make it at home. Yet some people believe that homemade ice cream is better than anything you can buy in a store. Of course, there was a time when people had no choice but to make their own. Homes and stores did not have freezers. So it was not possible to store frozen food. Instead people made ice cream at home and ate it immediately. Making ice cream took time and effort. Because of the work involved, people did not often make it.

After refrigeration was invented, companies began to produce ice cream for sale. To the next generation of children, store-bought ice cream was the *only* kind of ice cream. Still, some people remembered the delicious taste of homemade ice cream. Others looked back on the fun of churning—rapidly stirring back and forth—ice cream. Today, homemade ice cream has become popular again among ice-cream lovers. If

In this advertisement for a Peerless ice cream freezer a salesman demonstrates its use to a customer. The engraving dates to about 1890.

1

you have never tried homemade ice cream, you probably will after you read Becky Rupp's article!

"The Icing of the Cream" is an example of informative nonfiction. It presents information about the history and science of making ice cream. It is also instructional; it teaches you how to make ice cream.

ABOUT THE AUTHOR

Becky Rupp was born in 1948 in Burlington, Vermont. She began her writing career in 1983. Since then, she has published many magazine articles and several nonfiction books. She says that she knew she wanted to be a writer as early as the third or fourth grade.

In college Rupp found that she was interested in science. She majored in biology and eventually received a Ph.D. (Doctor of Philosophy) degree in biology. She worked as a research cell biologist and wrote articles for scientific journals. After the birth of her first child, Rupp wanted to work at home. She decided to use her talent as a writer. She asked the editors at *Country Journal*, whether they wanted to buy an article she was writing about squirrels. When they said yes, Rupp's career as a writer began. The topics she has written about include sleigh bells, butter, kites, home schooling, scarecrows, tree houses, vegetables, and blue jeans.

Rupp gets many ideas for articles from things she wants to learn more about. She says that what she likes best about writing articles is the research. "I like trivia," she says, "and learning about little chunks of stuff."

ABOUT THE LESSONS

The lessons that follow "The Icing of the Cream" focus on an author's purpose in writing. When writing a piece of nonfiction, an author may have a single purpose or may have more than one purpose in mind.

In the lessons in this unit you will learn about the different purposes nonfiction writers have for writing, and you will examine the specific purposes Becky Rupp had for writing her article.

WRITING: DEVELOPING AN INSTRUCTIONAL ARTICLE

In this unit you will learn how to develop and then write an instructional article on how to do or make something. The following suggestions will help you get started:

- Have you ever wondered how to play a video game, make an origami decoration, ice skate, bake a loaf of bread, work with clay, or paint a picture? If you have, you can probably find an instructional, or how-to, book about that or any other subject that interests you. Think about your hobbies or special talents. What do you enjoy doing in your free time. Do you play a sport? knit or sew? bake? draw? work on a computer? Perhaps you make the best pancakes in the world! You are probably an expert at something.
- List two or three favorite activities that you are knowledgeable about, do well, and would enjoy teaching to others.

AS YOU READ   Think about these questions as you read the article. They will help you identify Becky Rupp's purposes for writing it.

- What do you think was the author's purpose for writing the article?
- What kind of information does the author give you?
- Does the author teach you anything in the article? If so, what?
- In what ways does the author try to make the article entertaining?

The Icing of the Cream

Celebrate the dog days of summer by making your own ice cream

by Becky Rupp

Americans eat twice as much ice cream as anybody else in the world. On a regional basis, some of us eat even more than that. The top United States ice-cream consumers, who live in Alaska and New England, slurp up something on the order of seven gallons apiece annually—nearly twice the national average. Chances are that at least half of what they eat is vanilla, the all-time national flavor favorite. The second most popular is chocolate, followed by strawberry. After that just about anything goes: coffee is a biggie in Rhode Island, inhabitants of western Massachusetts like butter pecan, and Midwesterners are said to pitch for Rocky Road. I like peppermint stick, which, though far down on the national list of preferred ice cream flavors, is a great way to get rid of candy canes left over from Christmas. Still, as homemade ice cream makers, our family tends to stick to vanilla, chocolate, and strawberry. There's a lot to be said for sure bets.

Early Ice Cream

Chocolate of a sort may have been among the earliest ice-cream flavors. Legend has it that the Aztec emperor Montezuma ate an ice-cream-like dish of hot chocolate poured over snow. Early Mexican chocolate, however, was mixed with chili peppers and vanilla, and dyed orange—

hardly the delectable[1] dark-brown sweet we all know and love. The ancient Chinese ate a frozen rice-and-milk dessert flavored with camphor,[2] a possible relative of the ice cream brought back to Venice by Marco Polo in 1295. And the Romans ate fruit juice mixed with snow brought down by runners from the Alps.

Early ice cream was fairly sloppy stuff. It only became fully freezable in 1550 when Blasius Villafranca, an inventive Spanish doctor living in Rome, discovered that the freezing point of water could be lowered by adding salt to ice. Using the salt technique, the Italians became the world's first large-scale producers of ice cream and busily set about promoting their new treat all over Europe. Initially, ice cream was reserved for the nobility, and methods for making it were jealously guarded. Charles I of England went so far as to execute a loose-lipped palace chef who revealed the royal recipe.

Nothing, however, remains safe from the peasants for long. Ice cream made it to the uncivilized wilds of America by the mid-1700s, probably along with immigrants from France. Its first official colonial mention was in a letter written in 1744 by William Black, who had been served some strawberry ice cream while a guest of the governor of Maryland. George Washington was an ice cream lover, as was Thomas Jefferson, who brought an ice cream machine home with him from France in 1789, along with a recipe so outrageously complicated that it required eighteen separate operations from start to frozen finish. (Jefferson liked his ice cream encased in warm pastry crust, perhaps the first Baked Alaska.[3]) Mad Anthony Wayne[4] ate ice cream to celebrate his victory over

[1] very pleasing; delicious

[2] a strong-smelling substance that comes from the wood and bark of the camphor tree

[3] a dessert made of ice cream topped with beaten egg whites and quickly browned in an oven

[4] an officer in the American Revolution, called "mad" because of his daring deeds

the Indians at the Battle of the Fallen Timbers, and Dolley Madison[5]—"The First Lady of Ice Cream"—served a mountain of it (pink) at her husband's second inaugural ball, made with cream from the president's own dairy.

The Ingredients

The original ice creams, like the best homemade varieties today, contained only cream, sugar, flavorings, and occasionally eggs. The prime ingredient was and still is cream. The kind of cream used determines the richness of the final product. The most spectacular ice creams are made from heavy whipping cream (about 35 percent butterfat); lesser grades are made with light cream (20 percent), half-and-half (12 percent), or combinations of the above. Unfortunately, cream is also the most expensive ingredient, and the richer the cream, the more expensive it is. Cheaper ice creams can be made from substitutes such as condensed milk, and the ice cream industry uses a whole battery of noncream dairy products, including dried cheese whey. None of these ingredients tastes as good as cream, however, and the consensus[6] is that if you're going to ice something, ice the real thing.

The sweetener of choice, home ice cream makers generally agree, is granulated sugar. Alternatives such as corn syrups and artificial sweeteners alter ice cream flavors, sometimes unpleasantly. Recipes vary, but the rule of thumb is 3 to 4 tablespoons of sugar per 2½ cups of cream. It's best not to stray too far from this formula, because sugar also functions as an antifreeze: too little and the ice cream will be too hard; too much and it will be slush.

Some ice cream recipes call for eggs. Generally speaking the custard-type ice creams contain eggs, and the Philadelphia-style ice creams do not. French vanilla, which

---

[5] wife of James Madison, the fourth president of the United States

[6] general agreement of opinion

many people consider the richest vanilla on the face of the earth, is a custard ice cream. The eggless Philadelphia-style ice creams traditionally contain only pure cream, sugar, and flavorings. The name dates from the nineteenth century, when Philadelphia, with nearly fifty ice cream factories, was considered the ice cream capital of the world. (Today Pennsylvania is still one of the top ice-cream-producing states in the country, along with California and New York.)

Both types of ice cream recipes often require that the cream or custard base be cooked. In those cases, the ingredients should be cooled before adding flavorings because heat sometimes alters taste. This is particularly true of alcohol-based flavors: bottled vanilla extract, for example, which contains about 30 per cent alcohol; liquors; and liqueurs.[7] There are hundreds, even thousands, of different flavors of ice cream. On the market at one time or another have been banana daiquiri, bubble gum, casaba melon, eggnog, ginger fig, green tea, jellybean, maple, mincemeat, papaya, peanut-butter-and-jelly, prune, pumpkin, rhubarb, sunflower seed, truffle,[8] and violet—enough to make Baskin Robbins's famous thirty-one flavors (which, to be fair, vary from year to year) look positively pale. With a little imagination you can do it all at home. A good flavor to start with, fitting right in there between truffle and violet, is the all-American favorite, vanilla.

Real Beans

According to ice cream connoisseurs,[9] the best vanilla ice creams are made not with bottled extract, but with genuine vanilla beans. Vanilla beans are the fruit of a Central American orchid, an immense plant with vines up to 350 feet long. When ripe and ready for picking, the beans are 4 to 12

---

[7] liquor that has been flavored and usually sweetened

[8] a rare fungus used as a food and a flavoring

[9] experts on a particular subject

inches long and gold-yellow in color, stuffed full of the minuscule seeds that form the black specks in top-notch vanilla ice creams. Processing turns the original yellow pods into the skinny black beans sold in supermarkets and specialty shops. Vanilla was introduced to this country by Thomas Jefferson, who came across it during his diplomatic tour of duty in France. When he settled in as secretary of state in Philadelphia in 1790, Jefferson was appalled to learn that the City of Brotherly Love lacked vanilla beans. He promptly ordered a packet of fifty from Paris, perhaps then and there starting Philadelphia on the road to world-famous ice cream.

Most vanilla today comes from Madagascar. The beans cost about $1.50 apiece and can be used over and over until the flavor is depleted or can be slit open at once to release the seeds. It takes about three inches of bean to flavor a quart of ice cream. Unlike extract, the bean should be added to the cream or custard base while cooking, then fished out before freezing, rinsed, and stored for the next time around. If you can't lay your hands on real beans, at least make sure your vanilla extract is the natural product—it's distinctly better than the artificial vanilla now on the market, which is a benzaldehyde derivative. (The most commonly used vanilla substitute in ice creams is vanillin, a compound commercially derived from wood pulp treated with sulfuric acid.) Coffee, chocolate, and fruit purées can also be stirred in at the cooking stage. Fruit chunks, chopped nuts, raisins, and crushed candies should be tossed in later, part way through the freezing process when the mix is semisoft. These additions all lower the freezing point of the ice cream, which means that if added too early they slow down the whole process.

Ice Cream Machines

Ice cream freezers fortunately have improved a good deal since their early days. Martha Washington had to make do with a pair of pewter ice cream "pots," or interlocking bowls: the smaller, containing the ice-cream mixture, was rapidly twirled within the larger, which held ice and salt. Ice cream making remained at this awkward stage until 1846, when Nancy Johnson invented the hand-cranked freezer, a machine not too different in design from models on the market today. (She didn't patent[10] it, but two years later an alert entrepreneur[11] named William Young did. He kindly called the machine the Johnson Patent Ice Cream Freezer.) The basic ice cream freezer has three major parts: a metal can for the ice cream ingredients, a larger insulating wooden bucket to hold the can and its surrounding layers of salt and ice, and inside the can a multipaddled "dasher" or beater turned by a hand crank. In modern freezers the dasher is operated by an electric motor.

When you're ready to freeze, chill the ice cream mix, metal can, and dasher for at least an hour in the refrigerator. Once the mix is cold, transfer it to the metal can, filling it no more than three-quarters full. Ice cream expands as it freezes, partly because water expands as it solidifies and partly because the churning motion of the dasher whips air into the mix. Homemade ice cream usually expands only about 25 per cent, which means that it is generally more solid than the average store-bought product. Commercial ice creams are frozen in huge continuous-flow factory freezers which use liquid ammonia instead of rock salt and ice. In these, mixes solidify inside of 30 seconds, and air is subsequently pumped in mechanically, increasing the volume of the ice cream by as much as 50 per cent. It was once common practice among unscrupulous[12] manufacturers to balloon ice cream investments by pumping enormous amounts of air into their product. Today the Food and Drug Administration regulates the weight of commercial ice cream. By law, a half-gallon of ice cream must weigh at

---

[10] to get the exclusive right to produce or sell an invention or process

[11] one who organizes, manages, and assumes the risks of a business

[12] dishonest

least 2 pounds, 4 ounces, and the better brands weigh twice that amount or more.

Place the can filled with ice cream mix inside the outer bucket of the ice cream freezer and pack the intervening spaces with alternating layers of rock salt and ice. The salt-and-ice trick works because salt effectively lowers the temperature of ice water to 16–18°F, in contrast to the 32°F of unsalted water. Ordinary ice cubes will work here if enough of them come in contact with the sides of the metal container. Unfortunately, since ice cubes don't pack too well, enough of them usually don't. This in turn slows the freezing time, which can be a real problem, because if the cream mixture is churned too long you'll end up with butter. For efficient freezing, it's better to use crushed ice, easily produced by smashing ice cubes in a burlap bag with a baseball bat. (Snow also works well for winter ice cream making.) The salt of choice is rock salt, the chunky gray stuff used to sprinkle sidewalks in February. It is sometimes sold as "ice cream salt." Ice and salt should be layered into the bucket in a ratio of about 4 parts ice to 1 part salt. Some ice cream makers cut this ratio down to 8 to 1. One source recommends a 2-inch layer of crushed ice topped with a ¼-inch layer of rock salt, repeated to a point above the level of the ice cream mixture inside the can (not much higher, however; you don't want cold salt water in your ice cream). It's tempting to consider adding even more salt to further speed up the freezing process, but this is a trap: too much salt lowers the temperature too much, leading to uneven freezing inside the can. Only the stuff next to the walls, where it is coldest, freezes rapidly, while the mix in the middle remains soupy. It makes for lousy ice cream.

It should take about 20 to 30 minutes of churning, cranking at a rate of about 60 turns per minute, to freeze a quart of ice cream. At this point, according to one ice-cream expert, the mix should be about the consistency of stiff whipped cream—or even a little thicker, on the order of mashed potatoes. It must then be hardened, either by repacking the ice-salt layers and letting the mix sit, covered, in the shade for two or three hours, or by transferring it to the freezer compartment of the refrigerator (be sure to remove the dasher first). Some authorities feel that ice cream tastes better if it is allowed to "ripen" overnight, but we've never managed to wait that long.

A note of warning: once the ice cream is finished, be sure to clean the freezer thoroughly. Rock salt and ice is a corrosive[13] mixture and eventually will do the same awful things to the metal parts of your ice cream freezer that it does every winter to the underside of your car.

If you're not lucky enough to have grandma's old ice cream freezer, you can still buy one, hand crank and all, for about $20. Electric equivalents are somewhat more expensive, on the order of $30 to $50. Also available are even fancier models that can be filled with ice cream mix and placed directly in the freezer compartment of the refrigerator: no rock salt or crushed ice required. One drawback to these machines is that they generally have a much smaller capacity than the bucket-type freezers—usually only one quart, while the buckets hold four or six. Also they're a little too tidy for our taste. The really prime ice creams are made out in the backyard.

Fancy Ice Creams
At the frozen stage ice cream can be rippled or ribboned, which is a nice touch, particularly if you feel like being fancy. This is easiest to do if the ice cream is hardened in flat containers like loaf pans. It works only if the mix has set quite solidly and is hard enough to slice. To ripple you simply pour warm—not hot—rippling sauce in strips across the top of the ice cream and cut it deeply into the frozen block with a knife. Then rechill. The most common rippling sauce is chocolate

---

[13] capable of eating or wearing away

fudge, but good also are fruit syrups and sauces, butterscotch sauce, and coffee syrup.

In the Freezer

If you don't have an ice cream freezer, passable ice cream can still be made in shallow pans or trays in a standard freezer. The ingredients are the same, but the trick is to take the mix out periodically once it begins to set and beat it thoroughly, preferably with an electric mixer or blender. One ice cream maker suggests doing this every 30 minutes until the freezing is complete. The beating, like the constant churning of conventional ice cream freezers, prevents the formation of ice crystals which make the finished ice cream granular or sandy in texture. These same crystals turn old ice cream unpleasantly grainy. In this case the crystals accumulate as a result of "heat shock," an effect brought on by fluctuating[14] temperatures caused, for example, by frequently opening and closing the refrigerator door. Heat shock causes the tiny ice crystals in ice cream to melt and refreeze, each time becoming bigger and grittier. Crystals any bigger than one thousandth of an inch can be detected by oral touch receptors, causing ice cream to give an awful-feeling crunch when eaten. To prevent this, commercial ice creams contain stabilizers such as guar gums and carrageen, substances much more benign than they sound. In the absence of stabilizers, you can either learn to live with an occasional crunch, or you can eat your ice cream in one fell swoop. In the latter case, recommended by many, it's often helpful to point out that you are not a pig, just a texture purist.

Dish, Cone, or Soda?

Homemade ice cream freezes harder than the commercial varieties and is best thawed somewhat before serving. For half a gallon, 15 to 20 minutes usually does the trick. The best scooping temperature for ice cream is 8°F, at which point

---

[14] shifting back and forth uncertainly

you're all set for a dandy dish, cone, soda, or sundae. I've always preferred the cone, because there's nothing left over to wash up afterward. No one is certain who invented the ice cream cone, although everybody agrees that it first appeared at the St. Louis World's Fair in 1904. Among the rival contestants are the unnamed girlfriend of an ice cream salesman, a souvenir-stand owner named Abe Doumar, and a Syrian waffle maker named Ernest Hamwi. Hamwi, the story goes, had set up shop next door to an ice cream dealer who ran out of dishes, and Hamwi offered him some rolled waffles to use in their place. Two years later ice cream cones—called World's Fair cornucopias[15]—were on sale at Coney Island,[16] and by 1924, when a machine to mass-produce cones finally came along, Americans were eating more than 200 million a year. One of the advantages of the cone, along with its convenience (you can take it with you on the roller coaster), is that it's easy to lick. Licking is the best way to consume ice cream because the taste buds for sweetness are located at the tip of the tongue.

If you want your ice cream in fancier form than the simple cone, there are ice cream sodas and ice cream sundaes, ever-popular examples of our irresistible urge to improve upon a good thing. The traditional ice cream soda contains, in sequence, two tablespoons of flavored syrup, soda water, and a scoop of ice cream. You're not supposed to spoon it, but sip it slowly through a straw. One of the all-time soda greats is the Brown Cow: two tablespoons of chocolate syrup, Coca-Cola, and a scoop of vanilla. There's also a Black Cow, made with root beer. If sodas are too tame for your taste, the next step up is the sundae, which began its career as a soda-less ice cream soda. It was invented in the 1890s to circumvent a law prohibiting the sale of "stimulating beverages" on the Sabbath;

---

[15] horn of plenty, traditionally a goat's horn filled with fruits, to symbolize a good harvest

[16] a popular amusement park in Brooklyn, New York

the name is said to be a deliberate misspelling of "Sunday." Recipes for sundaes consist of ice cream decked out with syrups, fruits, nuts, candies, marshmallows, whipped cream, and anything else calorically disastrous that comes to mind. The champion sundae of all time was a 26,000-pound spectacular assembled and eaten in St. Albans, Vermont, in the glorious summer of 1983. It contained 3,000 gallons of ice cream topped with peaches, pineapples, strawberries, chocolate chips, peanuts from Jimmy Carter's[17] farm, and—you'll never guess—maple syrup.

While the caloric value of the average sundae is something only to be gingerly guessed at, the nutritional content of ice cream is a matter of record. Vanilla ice cream contains about 280 calories a cup, about twice as many as whole milk. Half of those calories come from butterfat. Commercial ice cream is required by law to contain at least 10 percent butterfat, but deluxe brands crank this up to 15 or 16 per cent, and homemade ice cream is even richer, around 18 per cent. While none of this bodes well for the dieter, there are some compensations. Vanilla ice cream is a reasonably good source of Vitamin A (twice as much as whole milk), calcium (about two thirds as much as milk), and protein (about half as much as milk). It also contains thiamine, riboflavin, and Vitamin B12—it's not *all* sin.

In the early 1800s, the aged, the delicate, and the very young were warned to abstain from ice cream in the belief that it brought on potentially dangerous digestive upsets. This credo,[18] like much of nineteenth-century medicine, has long since fallen by the wayside. It's common knowledge nowadays that ice cream is an excellent treatment for practically everything, from mild depression to heat prostration.[19]

And they say there's no such thing as progress.

---

[17] president of the United States from 1977 to 1981

[18] a statement of a belief or principle

[19] weakness, nausea, and dizziness caused by working too long in the heat

The recipe below makes about one quart of ice cream. You can increase it as necessary to suit the size of your ice cream freezer.

VANILLA ICE CREAM

1	quart light or heavy cream
1½	tablespoons vanilla extract or seeds from 3 inches of vanilla bean
¾	cup sugar
¼	teaspoon salt

Scald cream and seeds from vanilla bean. Remove from heat. Add sugar and salt while cream is still warm, stirring to dissolve. Chill in refrigerator for at least one hour. If using vanilla extract, add after the mix has cooled. Transfer to prechilled ice cream freezer and freeze as described in text.

REVIEWING AND INTERPRETING

Record your answers to these questions in your personal literature notebook. Follow the directions for each part.

REVIEWING   Try to complete each of these sentences without looking back at the selection.

Recalling Facts

1. The most popular ice-cream flavor in the United States is
   a. chocolate.
   b. vanilla.
   c. peppermint stick.
   d. strawberry.

Understanding Main Ideas

2. The discovery that made real ice cream possible was the
   a. invention of the electric freezer.
   b. discovery that cream becomes stiff when whipped.
   c. invention of electricity.
   d. discovery that salt lowers the freezing point of water.

Identifying Sequence

3. The first step in making ice cream is
   a. adding flavors.
   b. churning the mixture in an ice-cream freezer.
   c. layering the ice and salt in the freezer.
   d. choosing the kind of cream to use.

Finding Supporting Details

4. In the article which of the following is *not* given as an example of an ancient civilization that had a form of frozen dessert?
   a. Greek
   b. Aztec
   c. Chinese
   d. Roman

Getting Meaning from Context

5. "The beans cost about $1.50 apiece and can be used over and over until the flavor is depleted or can be slit open at once to release the seeds." The word *depleted* means
   a. used up.
   b. improved.
   c. made stronger.
   d. mixed.

INTERPRETING   To complete these items, you may look back at the selection if you'd like.

Making Inferences

6. On the basis of the article, you can infer that in years to come ice cream is likely to
   a. remain popular.
   b. have fewer ingredients.
   c. be eaten by more children than adults.
   d. be made only by hand.

Generalizing

7. People who make ice cream at home agree that
   a. sundaes are better than cones or sodas.
   b. artificial sweeteners are just as good as sugar.
   c. vanilla beans should be the only flavoring.
   d. cream is the key ingredient to good ice cream.

Recognizing Fact and Opinion

8. Which of the following is a statement of fact?
   a. The best vanilla ice cream is made with real vanilla beans.
   b. Salt lowers the freezing point of water.
   c. Ice cream that has a lot of air in it is the best.
   d. The really prime ice creams are made out in the backyard.

Identifying Cause and Effect

9. According to the author, licking is the best way to eat ice cream because
   a. it is the least messy.
   b. the tongue is sensitive to hot and cold.
   c. the taste buds for sweetness are on the tip of the tongue.
   d. the ice cream lasts longer.

Drawing Conclusions
10. From this article you can conclude that the author
   a. has probably made ice cream more than once.
   b. prefers to make vanilla ice cream.
   c. never eats store-bought ice cream.
   d. likes ice-cream sodas better than sundaes.

Now check your answers with your teacher. Study the questions you answered incorrectly. What skills are they checking? Talk to your teacher about ways to work on those skills.

Author's Purpose

Writers of nonfiction may have one of five purposes for writing. They may write to give information, to teach how to do something, to entertain, to express an opinion, or to persuade readers to do or believe something. Sometimes the writer may have more than one purpose in mind when writing a particular piece, although one purpose is usually the most important.

What purpose or purposes do you think Becky Rupp had in mind when she wrote "The Icing of the Cream"? Does she give the reader factual information about ice cream? Does she tell you how to make ice cream? Yes, she does both. Although those are her main purposes for writing the article, Rupp also hopes to entertain by making her article a pleasure to read as well.

In the lessons that follow, we will examine Rupp's purposes for writing her article and how she tried to achieve those purposes.

1. **Author's Purpose: To Inform** When the author's purpose is to inform, he or she will supply facts and information about a specific subject. It's important to consider the author's sources of information and whether the facts and information are correct.

2. **Author's Purpose: To Instruct** When an author's purpose is to instruct, he or she will provide instructions on how to do or make something. It's important that instructions be clear, complete, and in the correct order, step by step.

3. **Author's Purpose: To Entertain** Regardless of what other purpose or purposes an author may have for writing a particular piece of nonfiction, the author wants his or her writing to be entertaining for the readers.

LESSON 1   AUTHOR'S PURPOSE: TO INFORM

Before reading "The Icing of the Cream," did you know that the ancient Chinese ate a flavored frozen dessert made of milk and rice? Did you know that George Washington and Thomas Jefferson enjoyed ice cream? Those are just two of the many facts contained in Rupp's article. By including such facts, Rupp gives the reader information about the history of ice cream.

When you read factual information, you may wonder whether it is accurate. A *fact* is a statement that can be proved or disproved. Unless there is reason to suspect the author's motives for writing or to believe that the author was careless, you can usually assume that the information is accurate. Readers still may ask how or where the author found that information. Some authors supply their sources of information within the article. Others just present the facts.

After reading this selection, you may wonder how Rupp knew that George Washington loved ice cream. You may reason that Washington could have written about ice cream in a letter or a journal that Rupp read. Perhaps someone who knew Washington wrote about the president's taste for ice cream. Rupp does not state in her article where she found her information, but you can determine that such information must exist somewhere.

Read these two passages from the article. As you read, think about where Rupp may have obtained her information.

> Americans eat twice as much ice cream as anybody else in the world. On a regional basis, some of us eat even more than that. The top United States ice cream consumers, who live in Alaska and New England, slurp up something on the order of seven gallons apiece annually—nearly twice the national average. Chances are that at least half of what they eat is vanilla, the all-time national flavor favorite. The second most popular is chocolate, followed by strawberry. . . .

Ice cream made it to the uncivilized wilds of America by the mid-1700s, probably along with immigrants from France. Its first official colonial mention was in a letter written in 1744 by William Black, who had been served some strawberry ice cream while a guest of the governor of Maryland.

Look at some of the facts Rupp gives her audience in the first passage. She says that Americans eat twice as much ice cream as anybody else in the world; Alaskans and New Englanders eat about seven gallons apiece annually, nearly twice the national average; and the three favorite flavors are vanilla, chocolate, and strawberry. We can assume that the author did her research and that the information does exist and is correct. In order to check on the accuracy of her factual information, we need to know the source of her information or another source that contained the same information. Once a source is found, her facts could be proved.

Now look at the second passage. How does Rupp know that ice cream was made in America in the mid-1700s? Here Rupp includes her source. She got her information from a letter written by William Black in 1744.

EXERCISE ①

Read this passage from the article. Use what you have learned in this lesson to answer the questions that follow the passage.

Chocolate of a sort may have been among the earliest ice cream flavors. Legend has it that the Aztec emperor Montezuma ate an ice-cream-like dish of hot chocolate poured over snow. Early Mexican chocolate, however, was mixed with chili peppers and vanilla, and dyed orange—hardly the delectable dark-brown sweet we all know and love. The ancient Chinese ate a frozen rice-and-milk dessert flavored with camphor, a possible relative of the ice cream brought back to Venice by Marco Polo in 1295. And the Romans ate fruit juice mixed with snow brought down by runners from the Alps.

1. For which fact or facts does the author tell you the source of her information? Do you think the source or sources are reliable? Explain your answer.

2. Should you believe any facts Rupp presents for which she does not provide a source?

Now check your answers with your teacher. Review this lesson if you don't understand why an answer was incorrect.

 WRITING ON YOUR OWN

In this exercise you will use what you have learned in this lesson to add factual information about one of your favorite activities. Follow these steps:

- Review the list of favorite activities that you wrote for Writing: Developing an Instructional Article.
- Choose one of these activities for the topic of your instructional article.
- Copy the cluster map on page 23. Fill in the map with information, or facts, about your topic. If, for example, you chose to explain how to make origami birds, you would include facts about when you started your hobby, why it interests you, and a little history about the art of origami. On the lines extending from the circles, list important details. Remember, the facts you present should be correct. If in doubt, check your facts in a reference book before you list them.

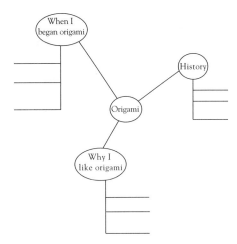

- Using the information in your map, write a two- or three-paragraph introduction that gives your readers some background information about your activity.

LESSON ②

AUTHOR'S PURPOSE: TO INSTRUCT

In "The Icing of the Cream," Rupp teaches you how to make ice cream at home. Instruction is a special kind of information: it tells you how to do or to make something. Cookbooks offer instruction. So do books and articles on computer programming, woodworking, and sewing.

There are three important standards for writing instructions. First, they should be clear. They should tell exactly what to do in simple, straightforward language. Second, they should be complete. They should not leave out even the most obvious step. Third, the steps in the process should be given in the order in which they must be followed.

Read the following passage from the recipe that appears at the end of article. As you read, think about how these directions meet the three standards for instruction.

Scald cream and seeds from vanilla bean. Remove from heat. Add sugar and salt while cream is still warm, stirring to dissolve. Chill in refrigerator for at least one hour. If using vanilla extract, add after the mix has cooled. Transfer to prechilled ice cream freezer and freeze as described in the text.

It is obvious that Rupp carefully thought out her instructions. First, they are clear—they tell you exactly what to do. Second, they are complete—even the most obvious steps are included. And third, they are ordered—steps appear in the order in which they must be followed.

EXERCISE ②

Listed below are the steps Rupp gives for making ice cream after the ice cream mix has been prepared. However, the steps are not listed in the order in which they should be followed. On a sheet of paper, list the steps in their correct order. You may look back at the selection in the section titled Ice Cream Machines if you'd like.

1. Churn the ice-cream mix for 20 to 30 minutes at the rate of about 60 turns per minute.

2. Transfer it to the metal can, filling it no more than three-quarters full.

3. Harden the mix, either by repacking the ice-salt layers and letting the mix sit, covered, in the shade for two or three hours, or by transfering it to to the freezer.

4. Place the can filled with ice cream mix inside the outer bucket of the ice cream freezer and pack the intervening spaces with alternating layers of rock salt and ice.

5. Chill the ice cream mix, metal can, and dasher for at least an hour in the refrigerator.

Now check your answers with your teacher. Review this part of the lesson if you don't understand why an answer was incorrect.

WRITING ON YOUR OWN ②

In this exercise you will use what you have learned in this lesson to write step-by-step instructions explaining how to do or make something. Follow these steps:

- The first step in writing instructions is to make a step-by-step outline of the process. Remember, just because you are familiar with the process doesn't mean that your reader is. If the activity you've chosen involves making something, be sure to begin your outline by listing the materials the reader will need to complete the project.
- Once you have made your outline of instructions, review it. Do your directions meet the three standards for instructions? 1) Are they clear? Have you used simple, straightforward language? 2) Are they complete? Have you included every step, no matter how obvious it may seem? 3) Are the steps in the process in the correct order in which they should be followed?
- Now, using your outline as a guide, write several paragraphs giving your instructions. You may want to use subheads to help your reader understand when a new section, or part, of the directions begins.

LESSON ③ AUTHOR'S PURPOSE: TO ENTERTAIN

"The Icing of the Cream" is a magazine article that first appeared in *Country Journal* magazine. An *article* is a written work that presents information about a topic. Magazines stay in business only if they satisfy their readers. For general-interest magazines, such as *Country Journal*, that usually means entertaining as well as informing readers. Readers want information, but if the author only presents a lot of facts, the article will not be very much fun to read. Readers expect to get some pleasure from reading an informative or instructional article.

Think about how Rupp entertains you in "The Icing of the Cream." One method she uses is including interesting facts.

Many people have learned about Marco Polo's visit to China, but how many people know that he returned to Venice with a recipe for ice cream? Even when Rupp is describing the process of making it, she includes entertaining bits of information. The reader does not need to know that information to make ice cream. It simply adds to the enjoyment of reading the article.

Two other methods that Rupp uses to make her article entertaining and enjoyable are talking directly to the audience and sharing her own experiences. She helps us feel her excitement and enthusiasm for making ice cream. By sharing her experiences and those of her family, she reassures us that we too can have fun. Like her, we can trust our own instincts when we make ice cream.

Rupp explains, for example, that according to some experts, once the ice cream is made it "tastes better if it is allowed to 'ripen' overnight, but we've never managed to wait that long." Clearly, the ice cream made in her home is too good to be left uneaten for a day. So she and her family happily ignore the experts and eat it up as soon as it is made.

She also adds to the friendliness of the article by talking about her own personal tastes, as well as those of her family. "I like peppermint stick," she says early in the article, after listing the general preferences of people in the United States.

EXERCISE ③

In this passage from the article, Rupp provides some interesting facts about the ice-cream cone and its origin. Read it and use what you have learned in this lesson to answer the questions that follow it.

> No one is certain who invented the ice cream cone, although everybody agrees that it first appeared at the St. Louis World's Fair in 1904. Among the rival contestants are the unnamed girlfriend of an ice cream salesman, a souvenir-stand owner named Abe Doumar, and a Syrian waffle maker named Ernest Hamwi. Hamwi, the story goes, had set up shop next door to an ice cream dealer who

ran out of dishes, and Hamwi offered him some rolled waffles to use in their place. Two years later ice cream cones—called World's Fair cornucopias—were on sale at Coney Island, and by 1924, when a machine to mass-produce cones finally came along, Americans were eating more than 200 million a year. One of the advantages of the cone, along with its convenience (you can take it with you on the roller coaster), is that it's easy to lick. Licking is the best way to consume ice cream because the taste buds for sweetness are located at the tip of the tongue.

1. How does the author try to entertain as well as inform in this passage?

2. What is Rupp's opinion concerning the best way to eat an ice-cream cone? What interesting piece of information does she provide to support that information?

Now check your answers with your teacher. Review this lesson if you don't understand why an answer was incorrect.

WRITING ON YOUR OWN ③

In this exercise you will use what you learned in this lesson to make your instructional article entertaining. Follow these steps:

- Reread the introductory paragraphs that you wrote for Writing on Your Own 1. Have you used any of Rupp's techniques? How could you make your introduction more entertaining?
- Rewrite your introductory paragraphs where necessary. If you haven't already, make your writing more entertaining by including an interesting fact or two about your topic that the reader doesn't *need* to know. Share a personal experience. Did something funny happen to you while you were learning about your activity? Maybe your first origami bird looked more like a dinosaur!

DISCUSSION GUIDES

1. Divide into two groups to prepare a class survey. One group will prepare questions for a survey to find out what the class's favorite ice-cream flavors are. The second group will write questions for a survey to find out which types—sundaes, cones, or sodas—the class likes best. Once your questions are complete, take the surveys. Share the results of both surveys with the class.

2. In small groups develop an advertising campaign that will introduce a new ice-cream flavor. Think of a name for your ice cream company and a name for the new flavor. Invent a slogan or a skit with dialogue that will promote your new ice cream. Present your ad campaign to the rest of the class.

3. Find out more about the facts that Rupp presents in her article. Form into small groups, each of which takes a different topic. For example, one group may want to research early forms of ice cream. Another may want to find out more about Blasius Villafranca and how salt lowers the freezing point of water. Another group may want to investigate the history of the ice-cream cone. Present the information from your research to the rest of the class.

WRITE AN INSTRUCTIONAL ARTICLE

In this unit you have learned how to develop an instructional article that will inform, instruct, and entertain. Now you will use what you have learned to write an instructional article that accomplishes those three purposes.

Follow these steps to complete your article. If you have any questions about the writing process, refer to Using the Writing Process (page 220).

- Gather and review the following pieces of writing you did in this unit: 1) a list of favorite activities, 2) the introductory informational paragraphs about your activity, 3) the paragraphs giving step-by-step instructions, 4) the revised introductory informational paragraphs.
- Reread your informational and instructional paragraphs. Do they read smoothly and make sense? Is there a smooth transition from your informational paragraphs to your instructional paragraphs? Make any revisions that you feel will improve your article.
- Write an appropriate title for your article. You may want to use a humorous title.
- Ask a classmate or friend to read your completed article, to follow your directions, and to actually do or make what your instructions direct. Ask him or her to comment on your article in general and your instructions in particular, and to suggest any ways in which you might improve either. If any suggestions seem valid, revise your article accordingly.
- Proofread your final draft for errors in spelling, grammar, punctuation, and capitalization. Make a final copy and save it in your writing portfolio.

Selecting and Organizing Facts

Jan Matzeliger and "The Real McCoy"

by Jim Haskins

INTRODUCTION

BUILDING BACKGROUND

Jan Matzeliger and Elijah McCoy were among the first African Americans granted patents. Matzeliger's complicated shoe-lasting machine made it possible to produce reasonably-priced shoes efficiently. McCoy was granted many patents, for everything from lubricating devices used on all types of machinery to an ironing table and a lawn sprinkler.

Have you ever thought about the inventions you use every day? Think about your routine each morning and try to list all the inventions you use. Most likely, you are awakened by an alarm clock. Next, you flip the switch in the bathroom, and the lights go on. You use the hot and cold water, brush your teeth, and comb your hair. Then you get dressed. Have you ever wondered who invented the machines that wove the cloth and stitched your clothes?

Now, what about breakfast? Perhaps you put a piece of bread into a toaster. Then you open the refrigerator and take out a carton of orange juice—which, by the way, is already squeezed. Now you glance at the clock and see that it's time to leave for school. In less than half an hour, you've probably used numerous inventions.

Who invented all the things we use every day? How do people get ideas for their inventions? It takes a creative mind first to recognize a problem and then to create a solution. Creating a successful invention is just the beginning, however. The inventor must then apply for a patent for the invention.

A *patent* is a government grant giving the inventor the sole right to make, use, or sell his or her invention, usually for a limited period of time. The first patent ever recorded in history for an industrial invention was granted in 1421 in Florence, Italy, to Filippo Brunelleschi, an Italian architect and engineer. That patent gave him a three-year monopoly to manufacture a barge with a special hoist used to lift marble.

In 1790 the United States Congress enacted the first U.S. patent laws. Under these patent laws, African-American slaves and freed slaves could patent their inventions; however it was often difficult for slaves to actually receive patents on their inventions. The slaves' owners often claimed the inventions as their own.

In 1858 the government took away the rights of slaves to patent their work. This came about when a slave owner named Oscar Stuart tried to patent a design for a mechanical cotton scraper in his name. The invention had really been designed by his slave, Ned. The United States government denied Stuart's application. Stuart then applied for a patent in Ned's name. Now the issue of permitting slaves to patent their inventions came to the attention of the government. A law was passed that denied slaves the right to patent their designs. The reasoning was that slaves were not citizens, and noncitizens could not patent their work. Finally, by 1868, with the passage of the Thirteenth and Fourteenth Amendments, African Americans were made citizens of the United States and could therefore apply for patents for their inventions.

In this unit you will read about two African-American inventors whose inventions have made significant contributions to society.

ABOUT THE AUTHOR

Jim Haskins's first book, *Diary of a Harlem Schoolteacher*, was published in 1969. At the time, Haskins was teaching a special-education class in Harlem in New York City. A social worker gave him a diary and suggested that he record his experiences and feelings about teaching disadvantaged students. Following the success of that book, Haskins was approached by other publishers about writing a series of books for young adults. Haskins knew what he wanted to write about: "books about important black people so that students could understand the larger world around them through books written on a level they could understand." Haskins has written more than 80 nonfiction books.

ABOUT THE LESSONS

The lessons that follow "Jan Matzeliger and 'The Real McCoy' " focus on how an author selects facts and then organizes them in an article.

"Jan Matzeliger and 'The Real McCoy' " comes from the book *Outward Dreams, Black Inventors and Their Inventions*. It contains a series of articles about African-American inventors. Because Haskins's book contains articles about many African-American inventors, he chose not to write detailed biographies of each one but to focus instead on each inventor's character and accomplishments. Such a brief account of a person's life and character is called a *profile*. In order to write a profile, Haskins had to limit the number of facts he could include about each inventor. He then had to organize those facts carefully to accomplish his purpose.

WRITING: DEVELOPING A PROFILE

At the end of this unit, you will write a profile about a person you know. The suggestions below will help you get started:

• Choose a subject for your profile. The subject should be someone you admire. You may want to choose a friend, teacher, coach, or family member.

- What do you admire most about your subject? Does that person do volunteer work? Is he or she an outstanding scholar or athlete? Does the person have one or more character traits that you especially admire: kindness, generosity, fairness, honesty, bravery, open-mindedness, selflessness?
- List as many facts about your subject as you can.

AS YOU READ

Think about these questions as you read the article. They will help you understand how Jim Haskins selected and organized the information in his article.

- What facts do you learn about the lives of Jan Matzeliger and Elijah McCoy? What kinds of facts about their lives are not mentioned?
- Carefully read the introduction (the first four paragraphs). Why do you think the author included this information?
- What does the author tell you about the character of each inventor?
- How does the author let you know what he thinks of the two inventors?

Jan Matzeliger and "The Real McCoy"

by Jim Haskins

By 1870 the constraints[1] imposed before and during the Civil War on the patenting of inventions by blacks had been lifted. Patent applications by blacks increased from a trickle to a stream to a rushing flood over the latter half of the nineteenth century. The biased[2] views previously held against blacks—that they were intellectually inferior, childlike, and so on—were slowly eroding[3]. In 1894 Congressman George H. Murray, a former slave and a champion of black education, told his colleagues in the House of Representatives:

> We [blacks] have proven in almost every line that we are capable of doing what other people can do. We have proven that we can work as much and as well as other people. We have proven that we can learn as well as other people. . . .
>
> I hold in my hand a statement prepared by one of the assistants in the Patent Office, showing the inventions that have been made by colored men within the past few years. . . .

[1] the act of limiting or restricting

[2] prejudiced; unreasonable or unbalanced in judgment

[3] wearing away; eating into

This statement shows that colored men have taken out patents upon almost everything from a cooking stove to a loco-motive. Patents have been granted to colored men for inventions and improvements in the workshop, on the farm, in the factory, on the railroad, in the mine, in almost every department of labor, and some of the most important improvements that go to make up that great motive power of modern industrial machinery, the steam engine, have been produced by colored men. . . .

After concluding his address, Congressman Murray then read into *The Congressional Record* a list of ninety-two patents received by black inventors; eight of those patents were held by the Congressman himself.

Black inventors were making an impact upon American society that could hardly be ignored, and one such inventor, Jan Ernst Matzeliger (1852–1889), created a device that was so complex and advanced it could hardly be understood, let alone ignored. His invention affected everyone in their daily comings and goings, yet few knew his name nor how he had improved their lives.

In 1876 Jan Ernst Matzeliger arrived in Lynn, Massachusetts, from his native Dutch Guiana. The son of a Dutch father and Surinamese mother, Matzeliger looked to the United States for opportunity and wealth. Although he spoke little English, he was interested in mechanical things and was able to obtain a job in a shoe factory. There he became aware of the problem involved in "lasting" shoes.

For years, various inventors had tackled the problem of shoe lasting: shaping the upper leather portion of a shoe over the last (the shoe form) and attaching this leather to the bottom of the shoe, the sole. Various inventors had contrived crude shoemaking machines, but the final step in shoemaking, lasting, could not—it seemed—be done by machine; it had to be done by hand. Or so everyone thought.

Matzeliger secretly worked on the problem for ten years

and, during that time, made a number of machines that he thought might last shoes, but each one ultimately failed. Finally, in 1882, he built a machine that did indeed last shoes, but then he ran into another, unexpected problem. When he applied for a patent and sent his diagrams to the United States Patent Office, his machine was too complex for the officials to understand. An official from the Patent Office had to be sent from Washington, D.C., to look at Matzeliger's original model, and on March 20, 1883, Jan E. Matzeliger was granted Patent number 274,207.

Almost at once, Matzeliger's machine revolutionized the shoemaking industry. His machine increased production tremendously while, at the same time, cutting production costs and, subsequently, the retail price of shoes.

While Matzeliger's name became famous in the shoemaking industry, his own life changed little. He had arrived in Massachusetts alone and friendless and, for much of his life, he remained lonely. Initially he applied for membership in several churches, but was denied because of his color. He finally joined a young adult group where he made some friends, but he never married, devoting the majority of his free time to developing his shoe-lasting machine. Nor did he get an opportunity to enjoy fully the fruits of his labors and self-denial. Six years after he patented his machine, in 1889, Jan Ernst Matzeliger died of tuberculosis.

One contemporary of Matzeliger's who did live to enjoy the fruits of his own inventiveness—and whose name was to become a household word—was Elijah McCoy. McCoy's name is still remembered today and has become synonymous[4] with the ideas of perfection and quality. When we say that something is "the real McCoy," we are remembering Elijah McCoy whether we are aware of it or not.

Elijah McCoy (1843–1929) was born on May 2, 1843, in Colchester, Ontario, Canada, the son of two runaway slaves,

---

[4] having virtually the same meaning

fugitives who had escaped from Kentucky by way of the Underground Railroad.[5] After the Civil War, Elijah and his parents returned to the United States, settling down near Ypsilanti, Michigan. There Elijah attended school and worked in a machine shop.

McCoy, even as a boy, was fascinated with machines and tools. He was fortunate to have been born into an era that suited him perfectly, a time when newer and better machines were being invented—the age of the machine. Following the footsteps of steam was that new energy source, electricity, which opened up even more opportunities for the inventive mind.

McCoy's interest only deepened with the emergence of each new device. He decided to go to Edinburgh, Scotland, where the bias against his color was not so evident, and serve an apprenticeship in mechanical engineering. After finishing his apprenticeship, McCoy returned to the United States a mechanical engineer, eager to put his skills to work. But companies at that time were reluctant to hire a black man to fill such a highly skilled position. Prejudice was strong and the myth that blacks were intellectually inferior to whites persisted. Companies felt that McCoy could not possibly be as skilled as he claimed to be and, even if he were, the white workers he might have to supervise would never take orders from a black man. The only job he was able to find was as a fireman on the Michigan Central Railroad.

The job of fireman was hardly one that required the sophisticated skills McCoy had obtained. His duties consisted of fueling the firebox of the engine to "keep the steam up" and oiling the engine. The way train and other types of engines were built meant that it was necessary to stop the train periodically—or to shut down whatever engine was being used—so the moving parts could be lubricated. If the engines were not oiled, the parts would wear out quickly or friction would cause

---

[5] the system by which opponents of slavery secretly helped fugitive slaves to escape to the free states or to Canada before the Civil War

the parts to heat up, causing fires. Hand-lubricating engines was an inefficient but necessary procedure.

Many men or women, when faced with a repetitive,[6] essentially mindless task, might sink into an unthinking lethargy,[7] doing only that which is required of them and no more, but this was not true of Elijah McCoy. He did his job—oiling the engines—but that job led him to become interested in the problems of lubricating any kind of machinery that was in motion. For two years he worked on the problem on his own time in his own homemade machine shop. His initial idea was to manufacture the machines with canals cut into them with connecting devices between their various parts to distribute the oil throughout the machines while they were running. He wanted to make lubrication automatic.

Finally McCoy came up with what he called the "lubricating cup," or "drip cup." The lubricating cup was a small container filled with oil, with a stop cock to regulate the flow of oil into the parts of a moving machine. The lubricating or drip cup seemed an obvious invention, yet no one had thought of it before McCoy; it has since been described as the "key device in perfecting the overall lubrication system used in large industry today." With a drip cup installed, it was no longer necessary to shut down a machine in order to oil it, thus saving both time and money. McCoy received his patent for it on July 12, 1872.

The drip cup could be used on machinery of all types, and it was quickly adopted by machine manufacturers everywhere. Of course, there were imitators, but their devices were not as effective or efficient as McCoy's. It soon became standard practice for an equipment buyer to inquire if the machine contained "the real McCoy." So commonly was this expression used that it soon spread outside the machine industry and came to have the general meaning of the "real thing," of

---

[6] characterized by boring repeated action, doing the same thing again and again

[7] drowsy dullness; lack of energy

perfection. Nowadays if someone states they want "the real McCoy," it is taken to mean that they want the genuine article, the best, not a shoddy imitation. In 1872, of course, Elijah McCoy could not foresee that his name would soon be-come associated with the idea of perfection. All he knew was that the thing worked and worked well on machinery of all types.

The lubrication of machinery fascinated McCoy, and he continued to work in that area. In 1892 he invented and patented a number of devices for lubricating locomotive engines. These inventions were used in all western railroads and on steamers plying[8] the Great Lakes. Eventually McCoy would invent a total of twenty-three lubricators for different kinds of equipment and, in 1920, he applied his system to air brakes on vehicles.

During his lifetime, Elijah McCoy was awarded over fifty-seven patents and became known as one of the most prolific[9] black inventors of the nineteenth century. In addition to his patents on various kinds of lubricating systems, he also received patents for such "homey" objects as an ironing table (a forerunner of today's ironing board), a lawn sprinkler, a steam dome, and a dope cup (a cup for administering medicine). He eventually founded the Elijah McCoy Manufacturing Company in Detroit, Michigan, to develop and sell his inventions.

Until his death in 1929, McCoy continued working and inventing, sometimes patenting two or three new devices a year. Today, although many may not know who he was or what he did, his name remains to remind us of the idea of quality, and the steady, ceaseless roar of machinery is a paean[10] to his inventiveness.

---

8 making regular trips

9 abundant; producing a great deal

10 a song or hymn of joy or praise

REVIEWING AND INTERPRETING

Record your answers to these sentences in your personal literature notebook. Follow the directions for each part.

REVIEWING

Try to complete each of these sentences without looking back at the selection.

Recalling Facts

1. Jan Matzeliger came to the United States
   a. to escape prejudice.
   b. to become an inventor.
   c. for opportunity and wealth.
   d. to become a writer.

Understanding Main Ideas

2. The sentence that best summarizes this article is
   a. As attitudes toward blacks changed, black inventors were able to succeed.
   b. Black inventors could not succeed because of discrimination.
   c. "The Real McCoy" means the genuine article.
   d. Inventors should always patent their ideas.

Identifying Sequence

3. Soon after McCoy left Scotland, he
   a. settled in Ontario, Canada.
   b. moved to Ypsilanti, Michigan.
   c. worked as a mechanical engineer.
   d. found a job as a fireman.

Finding Supporting Details

4. Matzeliger did not have an opportunity to enjoy the results of his invention because
   a. he died six years after it was patented.
   b. someone else patented his invention.
   c. he was working on other inventions.
   d. he returned to Guiana.

Getting Meaning from Context

5. Companies at the time were reluctant to hire a black man to fill such a highly skilled position. In this context *reluctant* means
a. willing.
b. forbidden.
c. unwilling.
d. expected.

INTERPRETING   To complete these items, you may look back at the selection if you'd like.

Making Inferences

6. How do you think McCoy felt about the job of oiling the machines?
a. He resented the fact that he didn't have a better job.
b. He saw the challenge of solving a problem.
c. He did just what was required of him.
d. He wanted to leave his job and return to Scotland.

Generalizing

7. This article shows that the two inventors
a. were greatly admired by the public.
b. never gave up their goals.
c. felt that their education and training were wasted.
d. wanted to become famous.

Recognizing Fact and Opinion

8. Which of the following is a statement of fact?
a. All people are bored by repetitive work.
b. McCoy could not possibly have been as skilled as he claimed.
c. Matzeliger and McCoy were the greatest black inventors.
d. Matzeliger and McCoy were born outside the United States.

Identifying Cause and Effect

9. The continuous-action "drip cup" had an advantage over hand lubrication because
   a. it used less oil.
   b. it was safer for the employee.
   c. it permitted machines to continue to run, saving time and money.
   d. it prevented damage to the machine.

Drawing Conclusions

10. From this article you can conclude that the author
   a. admired the inventors for achieving their goals.
   b. wishes that he had been an inventor.
   c. is an inventor himself.
   d. is more interested in inventions than inventors.

Now check your answers with your teacher. Study the questions you answered incorrectly. What skills are they checking? Talk to your teacher about ways to work on those skills.

Selecting and Organizing Facts

When nonfiction writers such as Jim Haskins decide to write an article on a particular topic or subject, they must first decide on a purpose for writing the article. In Unit 1 you learned that writers may have one of several different purposes for writing. Haskins's main purpose for writing "Jan Matzeliger and 'The Real McCoy' " is to inform the reader about the accomplishments and characters of these two black inventors.

Next, writers must carefully research their topics or subjects to gather information. Usually writers gather more information than they will ever use in their finished article, so their next task is to select which facts they will use and which facts they will discard. They choose, from the facts they've gathered, only the ones that illustrate or support the main idea that they are trying to convey in the article. In addition, writers sometimes want to communicate an underlying message, called a *theme*, to the reader. After selecting the facts to include in their article, writers must organize them in a way that will not only support their main idea and their theme but will also interest the reader.

In the following lessons we will examine these steps in the process and see how Jim Haskins applied them in writing "Jan Matzeliger and 'The Real McCoy' ":

1. **Selection of Facts** The author carefully selects the facts to include in an article on the basis of his or her purpose for writing, the main idea of the article, and the underlying message, or theme, that he or she wants to convey to the reader.

2. **Selection of Facts and Author's Feelings** The author sometimes selects facts to support his or her own attitude and to demonstrate his or her feelings toward the topic or subject.

3. **Developing a Theme** Once the author has selected which facts to include, he or she must arrange those facts in a way that will support both the main idea and the theme and will interest readers as well.

LESSON ① SELECTING FACTS

In "Jan Matzeliger and 'The Real McCoy'," Jim Haskins presents only carefully selected facts about the two inventors. He could have written a detailed account of the lives of these two men, beginning with their childhood, but that was not Haskins's purpose. He wanted to focus on Matzeliger's and McCoy's abilities as inventors and the character they displayed in their lives.

After reviewing the facts that he had gathered, Haskins carefully selected those facts that would illustrate or support his main idea. Read the following passage from the article:

> By 1870 the constraints imposed before and during the Civil War on the patenting of inventions by blacks had been lifted. Patent applications by blacks increased from a trickle to a stream to a rushing flood over the latter half of the nineteenth century. The biased views previously held against blacks—that they were intellectually inferior, childlike, and so on—were slowly eroding. In 1894, Congressman George H. Murray, a former slave and champion of black education, told his colleagues in the House of Representatives:
>
> > We [blacks] have proven in almost every line that we are capable of doing what other people can do. We have proven that we can work as much and as well as other people. We have proven that we can learn as well as other people. . . .
> > I hold in my hand a statement prepared by one of the assistants in the Patent Office, showing the inventions

that have been made by colored men within the past few years. . . .

    This statement shows that colored men have taken out patents upon almost everything from a cooking stove to a locomotive. . . .

The author does not directly state the main idea of the article in this passage, but it is clearly implied and could be stated like this: "As attitudes towards blacks and black inventors began to change, black inventors were able to demonstrate their abilities and patent many inventions."

When you read nonfiction, it is important to carefully consider the facts that the author presents. Ask yourself why the author has included those particular facts rather than other information that might have been available about the topic or subject. By thinking about the author's selection of facts, you can better understand the author's purpose in writing the piece and the message he or she is trying to convey.

EXERCISE ①

Read this passage from the article. Use what you have learned in this lesson to answer the questions that follow the passage.

    While Matzeliger's name became famous in the shoemaking industry, his own life changed little. He had arrived in Massachusetts alone and friendless and, for much of his life, he remained lonely. Initially he applied for membership in several churches, but was denied because of his color. He finally joined a young adult group where he made some friends, but he never married, devoting the majority of his free time to developing his shoe-lasting machine. Nor did he get an opportunity to enjoy fully the fruits of his labors and self-denial. Six years after he patented his machine, in 1889, Jan Ernst Matzeliger died of tuberculosis.

1. How does the information Haskins gives you about Matzeliger in this passage differ from the information he gives about him in the rest of the article.

2. Why do you think Haskins chose to include this information about Matzeliger?

Now check your answers with your teacher. Review this lesson if you don't understand why an answer was incorrect.

WRITING ON YOUR OWN ①

In this exercise you will use what you have learned in this lesson to write a sentence stating the main idea you want to convey about the subject of your profile. Follow these steps:

- Review the list of facts about your subject that you wrote for Writing: Developing a Profile.
- On the basis of your list of facts, determine the main idea you want to convey about your subject.

  For example, suppose your subject is an athlete who has overcome a very serious knee injury to become an all-star player. The main idea of your profile might be stated this way: "Tom Adams overcame a serious knee injury and became an all-star player."
- Now write a sentence stating the main idea you want to make about your subject.

LESSON ② SELECTING FACTS AND AUTHOR'S FEELINGS

Why did Jim Haskins choose to write about Jan Matzeliger and Elijah McCoy? It seems obvious that Haskins admires and respects the inventors' resourcefulness, determination, and creativeness. Despite the hardships they faced and the injustice of discrimination, the two succeeded. They accomplished their goals, and their contributions changed and improved life in America. Although Haskins never directly says that he admires these two men and that they are an inspiration to him, he implies it by including facts that demonstrate his feelings:

In the following passage look for facts that demonstrate the author's feelings toward McCoy.

> Many men or women, when faced with a repetitive, essentially mindless task, might sink into an unthinking lethargy, doing only that which is required of them and no more, but this was not true of Elijah McCoy. He did his job—oiling the engines—but that job led him to become interested in the problems of lubricating any kind of machinery that was in motion. For two years he worked on the problem on his own time in his own homemade machine shop. His initial idea was to manufacture the machines with canals cut into them with connecting devices between their various parts to distribute the oil throughout the machines while they were running. He wanted to make lubrication automatic.

Haskins uses these facts to point out how conscientious McCoy was. Even though the job was a boring, mindless task, McCoy not only did what was required but tried to come up with a better way to perform the task. The author shows that McCoy was determined and persistent by including the fact that he worked on the problem on his own for two years.

Such facts demonstrate Haskins's feelings of admiration and respect for McCoy.

EXERCISE ②

Read the following two passages from the article. Use what you have learned in this lesson to answer the questions that follow them.

> Black inventors were making an impact upon American society that could hardly be ignored, and one such inventor, Jan Ernst Matzeliger (1852–1889), created a device that was so complex and advanced it could hardly be understood, let alone ignored. His invention affected everyone in their daily comings and goings, yet few knew his name nor how he had improved their lives.
>
> One contemporary of Matzeliger's who did live to enjoy the fruits of his own inventiveness—and whose name was to become a household word—was Elijah McCoy. McCoy's name is still remembered today and has become synonymous with the ideas of perfection and quality. When we say that something is "the real McCoy," we are remembering Elijah McCoy whether we are aware of it or not.

1. What facts can you find in the first passage above that demonstrate Haskins's admiration for Matzeliger?

2. What facts can you find in the second passage that demonstrate Haskins's admiration for McCoy?

Now check your answers with your teacher. Review this part of the lesson if you don't understand why an answer was incorrect.

WRITING ON YOUR OWN ②

In this exercise you will use what you have learned in this lesson to select facts that demonstrate your attitude or feelings toward the subject of your profile. Follow these steps:

- Review the list of facts you wrote for Writing on Your Own 1. Do some of those facts clearly demonstrate the feelings of admiration you have for the subject?
- Look back at the example in Writing on Your Own 1. What about Tom Adams might you admire—his skill as an athlete, his hard work and dedication to practice to make himself a better player, his bravery and determination in going through a long rehabilitation process to recover from his serious knee injury?
- Now think about your feelings toward your subject. What is it that you admire about him or her? Have you listed facts that support your feelings? If not, add some facts to your list that do.

LESSON ③   DEVELOPING A THEME

Before writing an article, a writer often chooses a theme. A *theme* is an underlying message, or central idea, of a piece of writing. The theme may be directly stated in a sentence or may simply be implied by the information the author includes.

In a nonfiction work, such as Haskins's article, the theme is the unifying idea around which the author organizes facts. How does the author determine a theme for his or her work? The author does not just invent a theme but rather identifies a theme within all the facts he or she has collected. After carefully studying all the facts that he had collected about Jan Metzeliger and Elijah McCoy, Haskins noted a recurring idea that the collected facts pointed to. That idea became the theme of the article. Although Haskins does not state the theme directly, he clearly implies, or suggests, it. The theme might be stated like this: "Jan Matzeliger's and Elijah McCoy's great ability and determination enabled them to overcome many obstacles and achieve success."

Remember that the theme of a piece of writing is different from its topic. The *topic*, or subject, of an article is what the piece is about. Haskins's article is about Jan Matzeliger and Elijah McCoy. The theme, however, states something meaningful about the topic.

Read this passage from the article. Note how the facts included by the author support his theme.

> McCoy's interest only deepened with the emergence of each new device. He decided to go to Edinburgh, Scotland, where the bias against his color was not so evident, and serve an apprenticeship in mechanical engineering. After finishing his apprenticeship, McCoy returned to the United States a mechanical engineer, eager to put his skills to work. But companies at that time were reluctant to hire a black man to fill such a highly skilled position. Prejudice was strong and the myth that blacks were intellectually inferior to whites persisted. Companies felt that McCoy could not possibly be as skilled as he claimed to be and even if he were, the white workers he might have to supervise would never take orders from a black man. The only job he was able to find was as a fireman on the Michigan Central Railroad.

McCoy was clearly excited and fascinated with each new device he saw. By reading between the lines, you can guess that McCoy realized that he would need a better education. He also knew that the education he needed would be nearly impossible to get in the United States. McCoy did not give up. Instead, he moved to Scotland to learn mechanical engineering. When he returned from Scotland, he was again faced with the obstacle of prejudice; but, again, McCoy did not give up. He took a job as fireman on the Michigan Central Railroad, even though he had been educated to tackle a much more demanding job. As the article continues, Haskins presents additional facts demonstrating that McCoy was determined to succeed despite the obstacles in his path.

EXERCISE ③

Read this passage. Use what you have learned in this lesson to answer the questions that follow it.

In 1876 Jan Ernst Matzeliger arrived in Lynn, Massachusetts, from his native Dutch Guiana. The son of a Dutch father and Surinamese mother, Matzeliger looked to the United States for opportunity and wealth. Although he spoke little English, he was interested in mechanical things and was able to obtain a job in a shoe factory. There he became aware of the problem involved in "lasting" shoes.

For years, various inventors had tackled the problem of shoe lasting: shaping the upper leather portion of a shoe over the last (the shoe form) and attaching this leather to the bottom of the shoe, the sole. Various inventors had contrived crude shoemaking machines, but the final step in shoemaking, lasting, could not—it seemed—be done by machine; it had to be done by hand. Or so everyone thought.

Matzeliger secretly worked on the problem for ten years and, during that time, made a number of machines that he thought might last shoes, but each one ultimately failed. Finally, in 1882, he built a machine that did indeed last shoes. . . .

1. What facts in this passage help support the theme of the article: "Jan Matzeliger's and Elijah McCoy's great ability and determination enabled them to overcome many obstacles and achieve success."

2. Think about what the information in this passage tells you about Jan Matzeliger's character. What words would you use to describe the character traits possesed by Matzeliger?

Now check your answers with your teacher. Review this lesson if you don't understand why an answer was incorrect.

WRITING ON YOUR OWN ③

In this exercise you will use what you have learned in this lesson to determine a theme for your profile. Follow these steps:

- Reread the list of facts you wrote for Writing on Your Own 1 and 2. Look for a recurring idea that those collected facts point to. That idea is the theme.
- Write a sentence stating your theme—the underlying message, or central idea, that you want to convey to readers. Returning to the example we have used in Writing on Your Own 1 and 2, you might state the theme this way: "Tom Adams exhibited tremendous bravery and determination in overcoming a serious injury and achieving success."
- Copy the spider map below on a sheet of paper. In the center, write your theme. Look again at your list of facts. Select those that support your theme and write them on the lines.

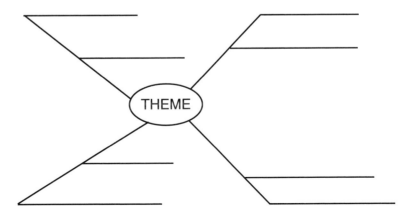

DISCUSSION GUIDES

1. Have you ever wondered how inventors think of their ideas? With the class look around your room and point out all the things that were invented to meet a specific need. As a class discuss what you think may have inspired the inventor to create each item. Look, for example, at the hinges that hold the door in place. Perhaps, long ago, someone got tired of moving a board that covered an entranceway. There was a need for an invention that would make a door swing open and then shut.

2. Think about what you have learned about the lives of Jan Matzeliger and Elijah McCoy. Now imagine that you could interview the two inventors. In a small group, write out the questions you would ask each man in your interview. Compare your interview questions with the rest of the class.

3. In a small group discuss the topic, inventions that we need. In your discussion think of inventions, not yet known to us, that would improve the quality of life—for example, a new kind of concrete or blacktop surfacing for roads and highways that would never freeze over. Think of how such an invention would increase driving safety. Make a list of your inventions and share them with the class.

WRITE A PROFILE

In this unit you have learned how to select and organize facts for an article or a profile that also develops a theme. Now you will use what you have learned to write a profile of someone you admire.

Follow these steps to complete your profile. If you have any questions about the writing process, refer to Using the Writing Process (page 220).

- Gather and review the following pieces of writing you did in this unit: 1) the list of facts about your subject, 2) the sentence stating the main idea you want to convey about your subject, 3) any additional facts that support your feelings about your subject you may have added to your list, 4) the spider map on which you wrote a sentence stating the theme of your profile and listing the facts that support it.
- Write a title for your profile. It should include the name of your subject.
- Write an introductory paragraph that includes the sentence stating the main idea of the profile.
- From the list of facts you've written, including those on the spider map, write several paragraphs to complete your profile. You should include your one-sentence statement of the theme in the second paragraph.
- When you have completed your first draft, read it carefully. Do the facts you've included support your main idea and your theme? Do the facts demonstrate your feelings of admiration for your subject?
- If possible, ask the subject of your profile to read it. If that is not possible, ask a classmate. Ask the reader to comment on your profile and to suggest any ways in which you might improve it. Revise your profile if you think it is necessary.
- Proofread your final draft for errors in spelling, grammar, punctuation, and capitalization. Make a final copy and save it in your writing portfolio.

Main Ideas and Supporting Details

Pompeii:
A Snapshot in Time

○

Excerpt from *Lost Cities and Vanished Civilizations* by Robert Silverberg

INTRODUCTION

BUILDING
BACKGROUND

Have you ever wondered where we get our information about people and cultures of the distant past? How do we know about the people of ancient Rome? How do we know that prehistoric people made tools? Where do the facts about these people come from?

Many of the facts come from archaeology. Archaeology is the scientific study of the people, customs, and life of ancient times. By studying the remains of ancient cities, including tools, weapons, pottery, and other such artifacts, archaeologists are able to form a picture of what life was like in the long-ago past. We know, for example, about ancient Roman people because archaeologists have found and studied Roman ruins. We also know about prehistoric people because archaeologists have unearthed sites where they once lived.

But how complete is our picture of the lives of ancient people? Imagine archaeologists a thousand years in the future uncovering the following articles from the present time: a wristwatch, a videocassette, a plastic cup from a fast-food restaurant, a skateboard, and a toothbrush. What conclusions do you think those scientists from the future could draw about

These petrified remains of a resident of Pompeii are a startling reminder of the tragedy that struck that Italian city on August 24, A.D. 79.

57

our lives in the present day? Any conclusions would be based only on the objects found. With so few remains to study, the archaeologists couldn't develop a very clear picture at all of what present-day life is like. For the same reason, modern scientists have generally not been able to get a complete picture of daily life in ancient times.

There have been occasional exceptions. Sometimes scientists have found much more than they expected. The selection you will read is about one of those exceptions. Nearly 2,000 years ago, within a 24-hour period, the ancient Roman city of Pompeii was completely buried under volcanic ashes when a nearby volcano erupted. Centuries passed, and the city and even its location were forgotten. Then, about 200 years ago, Pompeii was rediscovered. Since its rediscovery, archaeologists have been carefully excavating the buried city. They have found, preserved under tons of ashes, a picture—like a photograph frozen in time—of what life was like in this ancient Roman city.

The selection you are about to read, "Pompeii: A Snapshot in Time," is a chapter from Robert Silverberg's book *Lost Cities and Vanished Civilizations.* In the chapter, Silverberg describes how Pompeii came to be buried and how the buried city was rediscovered. He also tells how scientists were able to recreate in startling detail the lives of individual people who lived in ancient Pompeii.

ABOUT THE AUTHOR

Robert Silverberg (1935–) published his first short story at age 19 and his first novel at age 20. He is the author of more than 70 novels, nearly as many nonfiction books, and hundreds of short stories. He has won five Nebula Awards—the yearly award for the best science-fiction novel or short story—more than any other author. Fellow science-fiction author Isaac Asimov wrote, "Where Silverberg goes today, the rest of science fiction will follow tomorrow."

In the introduction to *Lost Cities and Vanished Civilizations*, Silverberg writes the following: "The story of archaeology is the story of a band of dedicated men, patiently laboring with pick and shovel under blazing suns. Archaeology is sweaty work. It is tiring work. It is slow work. The hours are long, the rewards often few and far between. There is nothing romantic about the day-to-day routine of archaeology. But the romance enters when the archaeologist's labors are done—when another of man's lost cities has returned from ruin and burial. The curtains of time are drawn back, and we see how men lived at the dawn of history. We share in their dreams, in their arts, in their accomplishments. . . ."

ABOUT THE LESSONS

The lessons that follow "Pompeii: A Snapshot in Time" focus on main ideas and supporting details in an informative piece of nonfiction writing.

In this selection author Silverberg provides information about the terrible disaster that destroyed the ancient city of Pompeii in a single day. He also gives details about the people and the daily life of Pompeii. Silverberg, like all good nonfiction writers, not only wants his readers to be able to understand the information he presents, but he also wants to hold their interest as they read the selection.

In this unit you will learn how the author used main ideas and supporting details to organize the information he presents in "Pompeii: A Snapshot in Time" so that it is both understandable and interesting.

WRITING: DEVELOPING AN INFORMATIVE ARTICLE

At the end of this unit you will write an informative article about a place that is familiar to you. The suggestions on the next page will help you get started:

- An informative article provides information about a subject. For your informative article you will use your own life as a source of information. Think about several places with which you are very familiar. Choose only places you have positive feelings about—places in the present where you feel comfortable or happy, or places from your past that bring pleasant memories to mind. One such place might be your own home or apartment; another might be the gym or athletic field where you play a sport. Perhaps you have good feelings about someone else's home, the local library, or a favorite picnic spot. Or you may have pleasant memories of a place from your past that you haven't been to in a long time—a summer camp or perhaps a place where you used to live or visit.
- Make a list of several of your favorite places.
- Now try to recall as many specific details as you can about each place. Just as author Silverberg does in his selection, you will want to try to include details that appeal to as many of the senses as you can: sight, sound, smell, touch, and taste. Make notes of several details about each place you have on your list.

AS YOU READ   Think about these questions as you read "Pompeii: A Snapshot in Time." They will help you look for the main ideas and supporting details in the selection, as well as help you see how those ideas and details are organized and presented.

- What is the overall main idea of this selection? Does Silverberg directly state this main idea, or is it only implied?
- How does Silverberg support his overall idea? What kinds of details does he give?
- How does Silverberg organize the main ideas and their supporting details?

Pompeii:
A Snapshot in Time

Excerpt from *Lost Cities and Vanished Civilizations* by Robert Silverberg

Not very far from Naples a strange city sleeps under the hot Italian sun. It is the city of Pompeii, and there is no other city quite like it in all the world. No one lives in Pompeii but crickets and beetles and lizards, yet every year thousands of people travel from distant countries to visit it.

Pompeii is a dead city. No one has lived there for nearly 2,000 years—not since the summer of the year A.D. 79, to be exact.

Until that year Pompeii was a prosperous city of 25,000 people. Nearby was the Bay of Naples, an arm of the blue Mediterranean. Rich men came down from wealthy Rome, 125 miles to the north, to build luxurious seaside villas. Fertile farmlands occupied the fields surrounding Pompeii. Rising sharply behind the city was the 4,000-foot bulk of Mount Vesuvius, a grass-covered slope where the shepherds of Pompeii took their goats to graze. Pompeii was a busy city and a happy one.

It died suddenly, in a terrible rain of fire and ashes.

The tragedy struck on the 24th of August, A.D. 79. Mount Vesuvius, which had slumbered quietly for centuries, exploded with savage violence. Death struck on a hot summer afternoon. Tons of hot ashes fell on Pompeii, smothering it, hiding it from sight. For three days the sun did not break through the cloud of volcanic ash that filled the sky. And when the eruption ended, Pompeii was buried deep. A thriving city had perished in a single day.

Centuries passed . . . Pompeii was forgotten. Then, 1,500 years later, it was discovered again. Beneath the protecting shroud[1] of ashes, the city lay intact. Everything was as it had been the day Vesuvius erupted. There were still loaves of bread in the ovens of the bakeries. In the wine shops, the wine jars were in place, and on one counter could be seen a stain where a customer had thrown down his glass and fled.

Modern archaeology began with the discovery of buried Pompeii. Before then, the digging of treasures from the ground had been a haphazard and unscholarly affair. But the excavation of Pompeii was done in a systematic, scientific manner, and so the science of serious archaeology can be said to have begun there. Since the year 1748, generations of skilled Italian workmen have been carefully removing the ashes that buried Pompeii, until today almost four-fifths of the city has been uncovered. Visiting Pompeii nowadays is like taking a stroll into the past—into that far-off time when the Romans ruled the world and the Emperor Titus sat on the throne of the Caesars.

Other Roman cities died more slowly. Wind and rain and fire wore them away. Later peoples tore down the ancient monuments, using the stone to build houses and churches. Over the centuries, the cities of the Caesars vanished, and all that is left of them today are scattered fragments.

Not so with Pompeii. It was engulfed in an instant, and its people's tragedy was our great gain. The buildings of Pompeii still stand as they stood 2,000 years ago, and within the houses we can still see the pots and pans, the household tools, the hammers and nails. On the walls of the buildings are election slogans and the scrawlings of unruly boys. Pompeii is like

---

[1] something that wraps or hides an object

a photograph in three dimensions. It shows us exactly what a city of the Roman Empire was like, down to the smallest detail of everyday life.

To go to Pompeii today is to take a trip backward in a time machine. The old city comes to vivid life all around you. You can almost hear the clatter of horses' hoofs on the narrow streets, the cries of children, the loud hearty laughter of the shopkeepers. You can almost smell meat sizzling over a charcoal fire. The sky is cloudlessly blue, with the summer sun almost directly overhead. The grassy slopes of great Vesuvius pierce the heavens behind the city, and sunlight shimmers on the water of the bay a thousand yards from the city walls. Ships from every nation are in port, and the babble of strange languages can be heard in the streets.

Such was Pompeii on its last day. And so it is today, now that the volcanic ash has been cleared away. A good imagination is all you need to restore it to bustling vitality.

A Roman City

As its last day of life dawned, in A.D. 79, Pompeii found itself in the midst of a long, sleepy Mediterranean summer. It was a city several hundred years old. Its founders were an Italian people called the Oscans, who had built the city long before Rome had carved out its worldwide empire. Greeks from Naples had settled in Pompeii too, and the walls that surrounded the city were built in the Greek style.

For more than 150 years, Pompeii had been part of the Roman Empire. The Roman dictator Sulla had besieged and captured the town in 89 B.C. giving it to his soldiers and making it a Roman colony. By A.D. 79, it had become a fashionable seaside resort, an Atlantic City or a Miami Beach of its day. Important Romans had settled there. The great orator Cicero had been very proud of his summer home in Pompeii. It was a city of merchants and bankers too.

Pompeii had not had unbroken peace. Twenty years earlier, in the year 59, a contest of gladiators had been held in the big outdoor stadium of Pompeii. A team of gladiators from the neighboring town of Nocera had come to fight against Pompeii's best gladiators. Tempers grew hot as local favorites were pitted against each other in combat to the death. Men from Pompeii began to hurl insults at Nocerans. Words led to blows. Then daggers flashed. A terrible massacre resulted, in which dozens of Nocerans perished and only a few escaped.

Nocera appealed to Rome, and the Roman Senate issued a stern decree: the amphitheater of Pompeii would be closed for 10 years. No more gladiatorial games! It was like having our Congress declare that neither the Yankees nor the Dodgers could play baseball for a decade.

The ruling was considered a great tragedy in sports-loving Pompeii. But an even greater one was in store four years later, in A.D. 63, for an earthquake rocked the town. Nearly every building in Pompeii toppled. Hundreds of people died.

One who survived the earthquake of 63 was the banker, Caecilius Jucundus. He was a plump, well-fed man with a harsh smile and beady eyes and a big wart on his left cheek. At the moment the earth shook, Caecilius was in the Forum, the main square of Pompeii. Much business was transacted in the Forum, which was lined with imposing stone columns arranged in a double row, one above the other.

As statues of the gods and slabs of marble tumbled to the ground, fat Caecilius sank to his knees in terror. "If my life is spared," he cried to the heavens, "I'll sacrifice a bull to the gods!"

We know that Caecilius escaped—and that he kept his vow. For when he rebuilt his house after the earthquake, he added a little strip of marble above his family's altar, and on it was a scene showing the earthquake and depicting the bull he had sacrificed. Next to the altar the fat moneylender kept his treasure chest, crammed full with gold coins—and, facing it, a portrait of himself, wart and all.

Sixteen years passed after the dreadful earthquake of 63. Sixteen years later, signs of the catastrophe could still be seen everywhere, for the Pompeiians were slow to rebuild. The private homes were back in order, of course, but the big public places still showed the effects of the quake. The columns of the Forum remained fallen. The Basilica, or law court, still looked devastated. The Temple of Apollo was not yet restored to its former glory. Such repairs took time and cost a great deal of money. The Pompeiians were in no hurry. Time passes slowly along the Mediterranean coast. The columns could be rebuilt next year, or the year after next, or the year after that. In time, everything would be attended to. Commerce and daily life were more important.

But time was running short.

The Last Day

At dawn, on the 24th of August, in the year 79, Pompeii's 25,000 people awakened to another hot day in that hot summer. There was going to be a performance in the arena that night, and the whole town was looking forward to the bloody contests of the gladiators, for the Senate's ban had long since ended. The rumble of heavy wooden wheels was heard as carts loaded with grain entered the city from the farms outside the walls. Over the centuries the steady stream of carts had worn ruts deep into the pavement of Pompeii's narrow streets.

Wooden shutters were drawn back noisily. The grocers and sellers of fruit opened their shops, displaying their wares on trays set out on the sidewalk. In the wine shops, the girls who sold wine to the thirsty sailors got ready for another busy day. . . .

Outside, children headed toward school, carrying slates and followed by their dogs. Nearly everyone in Pompeii had a dog, and barking could be heard everywhere as the Pompeiian pets greeted one another. A small boy who had just learned the Greek alphabet stopped in front of a blank wall and took a piece of charcoal from his tunic. Hastily he scribbled the Greek letters: *alpha, beta, gamma* . . .

In the Forum, the town's important men had gathered after breakfast to read the political signs that were posted during the night. Elsewhere in the Forum, the wool merchants talked business and the men who owned the vineyards were smiling to each other about the high quality of this year's wine, which would fetch a good price in other countries. . . .

The quiet morning moved slowly along. There was nothing very unusual about Pompeii. Hundreds of other towns just like it dotted the rolling plains of Italy.

But tragedy was on its way. Beneath Vesuvius' vine-covered slopes, a mighty force was about to break loose.

No one in Pompeii knew the dangerous power imprisoned in Vesuvius. For 1,500 years the mountain had slept quietly; but far beneath the crest a boiling fury of molten lava had gradually been gathering strength. The solid rock of Vesuvius held the hidden forces in check. The earthquake 16 years before had been the first sign that the trapped fury beneath the mountain was struggling to break free. Pressure was building up. In the city at the base of the mountain, life went on in complete ignorance of the looming catastrophe.

Vesuvius Erupts

At 1 o'clock in the afternoon on the 24th of August, 79, the critical point was reached. The walls of rock could hold no longer.

The mountain exploded, raining death on thousands.

Like many tragedies, this one was misunderstood at first. Down in Pompeii, four miles from Vesuvius, a tremendous explosion was heard, echoing ringingly off the mountains on the far side of the city.

"What was that?" people cried from one end of town to another. They stared at each other, puzzled, troubled. Were the gods fighting in heaven? Is that what the loud explosion was?

"Look," somebody shouted. "Look at Vesuvius!"

Thousands of eyes swiveled upward. Thousands of arms

pointed. A black cloud was rising from the shattered crest of the mountain. Higher and higher it rose. An eyewitness, the Roman philosopher Pliny, described the cloud as he saw it from Misenum, 22 miles from Pompeii on the opposite side of the Bay:

"Better than any other tree, the pine can give an idea of the shape and appearance of this cloud," Pliny wrote in his notebook later that day. "In fact it was projected into the air like an enormous trunk and then spread into many branches, now white, now black, now spotted, according to whether earth or ashes were thrown up."

Minutes passed. The sound of the great explosion died away, but it still tingled in everyone's ears. The cloud over Vesuvius still rose, black as night, higher and higher.

"The cloud is blotting out the sun!" someone cried in terror.

Still no one in Pompeii had perished. The fragments of rock thrown up when the mountain exploded all fell back on the volcano's slopes. Within the crater, sizzling masses of molten rock were rushing upward, and upwelling gas drove small blobs of liquefied stone thousands of feet into the air. They cooled, high above the gaping mouth of the volcano, and plummeted earthward.

A strange rain began to fall on Pompeii—a rain of stone.

The stones were light. They were pumice stones, consisting mostly of air bubbles. They poured down as though there had been a sudden cloudburst. The pumice stones, or lapilli, did little damage. They clattered against the wooden roofs of the Pompeiian houses. They fell by the hundreds in the streets. The people who had rushed out of houses and shops to see what had caused the explosion now scrambled to take cover as the weird rain of lapilli continued.

"What is happening?" Pompeiians asked one another. They rushed to the temples—the Temple of Jupiter, the Temple of Apollo, the Temple of Isis. Bewildered priests tried to calm bewildered citizens. Darkness had come at midday, and a rain of small stones fell from the sky, and who could explain it?

Some did not wait for explanation. In a tavern near the edge of the city, half a dozen gladiators who were scheduled to compete in that night's games decided to flee quickly. They had trumpets with them that were used to sound a fanfare at the amphitheater. But they tossed the trumpets aside, leaving them to be found centuries later. Covering their heads with tiles and pieces of wood, the gladiators rushed out into the hail of lapilli and sprinted toward the open country beyond the walls, where they hoped they would be safe.

Vesuvius was rumbling ominously, now. The sky was dark. Lapilli continued to pour down, until the streets began to clog with them.

"The eruption will be over soon!" a hopeful voice exclaimed.

But it did not end. An hour went by and darkness still shrouded everything, and still the lapilli fell. All was confusion now. Children struggled home from school, panicky in the midday darkness.

The people of Pompeii knew that doom was at hand, now. Their fears were doubled when an enormous rain of hot ashes began to fall on them, along with more lapilli. Pelted with stones, half smothered by the ashes, the Pompeiians cried out to the gods for mercy. The wooden roofs of some of the houses began to catch fire as the heat of the ashes reached them. Other buildings were collapsing under the weight of the pumice stones that had fallen on them.

In those first few hours, only the quick-witted managed to escape. Vesonius Primus, the wealthy wool merchant, called his family together and piled jewelry and money into a sack. Lighting a torch, Vesonius led his little band out into the nightmare of the streets. Overlooked in the confusion was Vesonius' black watchdog, chained in the courtyard. The terrified dog barked wildly as lapilli struck and drifting white ash settled around him. The animal struggled with his chain, battling fiercely to get free, but the chain held, and no one heard the dog's cries. The humans were too busy saving themselves.

Many hundreds of Pompeiians fled in those first few dark hours. Stumbling in the darkness, they made their way to the city gates, then out, down to the harbor. They boarded boats and got away, living to tell the tale of their city's destruction. Others preferred to remain within the city, huddling inside the temples, or in the public baths, or in the cellars of their homes. They still hoped that the nightmare would end—that the tranquillity of a few hours ago would return. . . .

It was evening, now. And new woe was in store for Pompeii. The earth trembled and quaked! Roofs that had somehow withstood the rain of lapilli went crashing in ruin, burying hundreds who had hoped to survive the eruption. In the Forum, tall columns toppled as they had in 63. Those who remembered that great earthquake screamed in new terror as the entire city seemed to shake in the grip of a giant fist.

Three feet of lapilli now covered the ground. Ash floated in the air. Gusts of poisonous gas came drifting from the belching crater, though people could still breathe. Roofs were collapsing everywhere. The cries of the dead and dying filled the air. Rushing throngs,[2] blinded by the darkness and the smoke, hurtled madly up one street and down the next, trampling the fallen in a crazy, fruitless dash toward safety. Dozens of people plunged into dead-end streets and found themselves trapped by crashing buildings. They waited there, too frightened to run farther, expecting the end.

The rich man Diomedes was another of those who decided not to flee at the first sign of alarm. Rather than risk being crushed by the screaming mobs, Diomedes calmly led the members of his household into the solidly built basement of his villa. Sixteen people altogether, as well as his daughter's dog and her beloved little goat. They took enough food and water to last for several days.

---

[2] large groups or crowds

But for all his shrewdness and foresight, Diomedes was undone anyway. Poison gas was creeping slowly into the underground shelter! He watched his daughter begin to cough and struggle for breath. Vesuvius was giving off vast quantities of deadly carbon monoxide, that was now settling like a blanket over the dying city. . . .

The poison gas thickened as the terrible night continued. It was possible to hide from the lapilli, but not from the gas, and Pompeiians died by the hundreds. Carbon monoxide gas keeps the body from absorbing oxygen. Victims of carbon monoxide poisoning get sleepier and sleepier, until they lose consciousness, never to regain it. All over Pompeii, people lay down in the beds of lapilli, overwhelmed by the gas, and death came quietly to them. . . .

Two prisoners, left behind in the jail when their keepers fled, pounded on the sturdy wooden doors. "Let us out!" they called. But no one heard, and the gas entered. They died, not knowing that the jailers outside were dying as well.

In a lane near the Forum, a hundred people were trapped by a blind-alley wall. Others hid in the stoutly built public bathhouses, protected against collapsing roofs but not against the deadly gas. Near the house of Diomedes, a beggar and his little goat sought shelter. The man fell dead a few feet from Diomedes' door; the faithful goat remained by his side, its silver bell tinkling, until its turn came.

All through the endless night, Pompeiians wandered about the streets or crouched in their ruined homes or clustered in the temples to pray. By morning, few remained alive. Not once had Vesuvius stopped hurling lapilli and ash into the air, and the streets of Pompeii were filling quickly. At midday on August 25, exactly 24 hours after the beginning of the holocaust,[3] a second eruption racked the volcano. A second cloud of ashes rose above Vesuvius' summit. The wind blew ash as far as Rome and Egypt. But most of the new ashes descended on Pompeii.

---

[3] a great or total destruction, often by fire

The deadly shower of stone and ashes went unslackening into its second day. But it no longer mattered to Pompeii whether the eruption continued another day or another year. For by midday on August 25, Pompeii was a city of the dead. . . .

Pompeii Uncovered

Arriving at Pompeii today, you leave your car outside and enter through an age-old gate. Just within the entrance is a museum that has been built in recent years to house many of the smaller antiquities found in the ruins. Here are statuettes and toys, saucepans and loaves of bread. The account books of the banker Caecilius Jucundus are there, noting all the money he had lent at steep interest rates. Glass cups, coins, charred beans and peas, and turnips, baskets of grapes and plums and figs, a box of chestnuts—the little things of Pompeii have all been miraculously preserved for your startled eyes.

Then you enter the city proper. The streets are narrow and deeply rutted with the tracks of chariot wheels. Only special narrow Pompeiian chariots could travel inside the town. Travelers from outside were obliged to change vehicles when they reached the walls of the city. This provided a profitable monopoly[4] for the Pompeiian equivalent of cabdrivers, 20 centuries ago!

At each intersection, blocks of stone several feet high are mounted in the roadway, so designed that chariot wheels could pass on either side of them.

"Those are steppingstones for the people of Pompeii," your guide tells you. "Pompeii had no sewers, and during heavy rainfalls the streets were flooded with many inches of water. The Pompeiians could keep their feet dry by walking on those stones." . . .

The houses and shops are of stone. The upper stories, which were wooden, were burned away in the holocaust or

---

[4] exclusive control or possession of something; goods or a service controlled by one party

simply crumbled with the centuries. The biggest of the shops are along the Street of Abundance, which must have been the Fifth Avenue of its day. Silversmiths, shoemakers, manufacturers of cloth—all had their shops here. And every few doors, there is another thermopolium, or wine shop. In many of these, the big jars of wine are still intact, standing in holes in marble counters just the way bins of ice cream are stored in a soda fountain today. . . .

The center of the city's life was the Forum, a large square which you enter not far from the main gate of the city. Before the earthquake of 63, Pompeii's Forum must have been a truly imposing place, enclosed on three sides by a series of porticoes[5] supported by huge columns. At the north end, on the fourth side, stood the temple of Jupiter, Juno, and Minerva, raised on a podium 10 feet high. But the earthquake toppled the temple and most of the columns, and not much rebuilding had been done at the time of the eruption. Pompeii's slowness to rebuild was our eternal loss, for little remains of the Forum except the stumps of massive columns. . . .

Other public buildings were also on the main square: the headquarters of the wool industry, and several other temples, including one dedicated to Vespasian (father of Titus), a Roman emperor who was worshipped as a deity.[6] Near the Forum was a macellum, or market, where foodstuffs were sold and where beggars wandered.

Pompeii had many beggars. One of them was found in April, 1957, at the gate of the road leading to the town of Nocera. A cast taken of him shows him to have been less than 5 feet tall, and deformed by the bone disease known as rickets. On the last day of Pompeii's life, this beggar had gone about asking for alms, and some generous citizen had given him a bone with a piece of meat still adhering[7] to it. When

---

[5] porches or walkways having roofs supported by columns

[6] a god or a goddess

[7] holding fast to or sticking to

the eruption came, the beggar tried to flee, jealously guarding his precious sack containing the cutlet—and he was found with it, 2,000 years later.

Pompeii was a city of many fine temples, both around the Forum and in the outlying streets. One of the most interesting is one dating from the sixth century B.C., the oldest building in the city. Only the foundation and a few fragmented columns remain, but this temple was evidently regarded with great reverence, since it was located in the center of a fairly large triangular space adjoining the main theater. Nearby is the Temple of Isis, which was rebuilt after the earthquake and so is in fairly good preservation. Isis, an Egyptian goddess, was one of the many foreign gods and goddesses who had come to be worshipped in the Roman Empire by the time of the destruction of Pompeii. Her gaudily decorated temple at Pompeii is the only European temple of Isis that has come down to us from the ancient world.

But many temples, bathhouses, amphitheaters, and government buildings have survived in other places. What makes Pompeii uniquely significant is the wealth of knowledge it gives us about the *private* lives of its people. Nowhere else do we have such complete information about the homes of the ancients, about their customs and living habits, about their humble pots and pans.

The houses in Pompeii show the evolution of styles over a period of several centuries. Many of the houses are built to the same simple plan: a central court, known as the atrium, around which a living room, bedrooms, and a garden are arrayed. This was the classic Roman style of home. Some of the later and more, impressive houses show the influence of Greek styles, with paintings and mosaic[8] decorations as well as baths, reception rooms, huge gardens, and sometimes a second atrium.

---

[8] a decoration made by sticking small, colorful pieces of material on a surface to make a picture or a pattern

The houses of Pompeii are known by name, and a good deal is known of their occupants. One of the most famous is the House of the Vetti Brothers, which is lavishly decorated with paintings, mosaics, and sculptures. The inscriptions on these houses are often amusing today. One businessman had written on the walls of his villa, WELCOME PROFITS! Another greeted his visitors with the inscribed words, PROFITS MEAN JOY!

At the so-called House of the Tragic Poet, a mosaic shows a barking dog, with the inscription *cave canem*— "Beware of the dog." On the building known as the House of the Lovers, which received its name because the newly married Claudius Elogus lived there, someone had written a line of verse dedicated to the newlyweds on the porch: *Amantes, ut apes, vitam mellitem exigunt.* ("Lovers, like bees, desire a life full of honey.")

The House of the Gilt Cupids had a garden filled with statuettes and a fishpond in the courtyard. The House of Menander, which belonged to Quintus Poppaeus, had recently been redecorated, and its wall paintings are particularly fine. (The house is known as the House of Menander because Quintus Poppaeus, a lover of the theater, had had a portrait of the Greek comic playwright Menander placed on one of the walls.)

One interesting house uncovered since World War II is the Villa of Giulia Felix ("Happy Julia") which was of exceptional size. Apparently Giulia found the expense of this elegant house too much for her budget, because she had opened her baths to the public and advertised the fact with a sign on the gate. For a fee, Pompeiians who scorned the crowds at the public baths could bathe at Giulia's in privacy and comfort. Even this income does not seem to have been enough, for another sign uncovered in 1953 announced that the magnificent villa was for rent. . . .

One of the truly fascinating aspects of Pompeii is the multitude of scribbled street signs. Notices were painted directly on the stone, and have come down to us. At the big amphitheater, an inscription tells us, "The troupe of gladiators owned by Suettius Centus will give a performance at Pompeii on May 31st. There will be an animal show. The awnings will be used." And at the theater where plays were given, a message to a popular actor reads, "Actius, beloved of the people, come back soon; fare thee well!"

There are inscriptions at the taverns too. "Romula loves Staphyclus" is on one wall. Elsewhere there is a poem that sounds like one of today's hit tunes: "Anyone could as well stop the winds blowing, / And the waters from flowing, / As stop lovers from loving." . . .

To enter Pompeii is to step into the Rome of the Caesars. An entire city, forever frozen in the last moment of its life by a terrible cataclysm,[9] awaits the visitor. Thanks to the painstaking work of generations of devoted Italian archaeologists, we can experience today the most minute details of life 20 centuries ago in a Roman city. So much do we know of the people of Pompeii that they take on vivid life for us—the banker Jucundus, the wool merchant Vesonius, the newlywed Claudius Elogus, the nobleman Diomedes. The dreadful eruption that snatched the life of these people and this city in a single day also gave it a kind of immortality. Pompeii and its people live on today, in timeless permanence, their city transformed by Vesuvius' fury into a miraculous survivor of the ancient world.

---

[9] a catastrophe that suddenly and violently occurs

REVIEWING AND INTERPRETING

Record your answers to these questions in your personal literature notebook. Follow the directions for each part.

REVIEWING

Recalling Facts

Try to complete each of these sentences without looking back at the selection.

1. The city of Pompeii was located in
   a. Greece.
   b. Egypt.
   c. Italy.
   d. Naples.

Understanding Main Ideas

2. In a 24-hour period, Pompeii was
   a. evacuated.
   b. buried by lava.
   c. burned to the ground.
   d. buried in ashes.

Identifying Sequence

3. Hot ashes fell on Pompeii
   a. after the pumice stones began to fall.
   b. before the pumice stones began to fall.
   c. after most of the citizens had fled.
   d. after most of the houses had burned.

Getting Meaning from Context

4. Many Pompeiians "hoped that the nightmare would end— that the tranquillity of a few hours ago would return." The word *tranquility* means
   a. sunlight.
   b. peacefulness.
   c. nighttime.
   d. celebrations.

Finding Supporting Details

5. Some Pompeiians did not leave the city because they
   a. thought they were safe in their houses.
   b. thought their gods would protect them.
   c. had survived earlier eruptions of Vesuvius.
   d. thought the world was ending.

INTERPRETING To complete these items, you may look back at the selection if you'd like.

Making Inferences

6. From the article, you can infer that
   a. a new city was eventually built on the ruins of Pompeii.
   b. efforts were begun immediately to dig Pompeii from the ashes.
   c. Mount Vesuvius will probably never erupt again.
   d. Pompeii is a popular modern tourist attraction.

Generalizing

7. When Silverberg writes, "To enter Pompeii is to step into the Rome of the Caesars," he means that
   a. the city of Rome was located on the site where Pompeii once was.
   b. the ruins of Pompeii show us what Rome must have been like during the same period.
   c. archaeologists have excavated buried ruins in Rome also.
   d. Pompeii was an ancient Roman city.

Recognizing Fact and Opinion

8. Which of the following is a statement of Silverberg's opinion?
   a. The center of the city's life was the Forum, a large square whose entrance was not far from the main gate of the city.
   b. Pompeii had many beggars.
   c. One of the truly fascinating aspects of Pompeii is the multitude of scribbled street signs.
   d. Many hundreds of Pompeiians fled in those first few dark hours.

Identifying Cause and Effect

9. Many Pompeiians died because
    a. Mount Vesuvius erupted in the middle of the day.
    b. the volcano gave off carbon-monoxide gas.
    c. they didn't have enough food or water.
    d. there was a wall around the city.

Drawing Conclusions

10. From what Silverberg writes in this selection, we can conclude that
    a. there has never been another catastrophe as bad as the destruction of Pompeii.
    b. archaeological excavations take a great deal of time.
    c. the majority of Pompeiians escaped the city unharmed.
    d. archaeologists have completed their work at Pompeii.

Now check your answers with your teacher. Study the items you answered incorrectly. What skills are they checking? Talk with your teacher about ways to work on these skills.

Main Ideas and Supporting Details

Author Silverberg studies archaeologists' work and their discoveries. Then he writes about what he has learned. He selects and organizes his information so that it can be understood and enjoyed by the general reader. "Pompeii: A Snapshot in Time" is filled with fascinating facts, but if Silverberg had not organized this information carefully, this selection would have been uninteresting and difficult to read—just a random collection of facts. The most common way a writer organizes a piece of informative writing is by presenting one or more main ideas and supporting them with details. The information in this selection is organized around one overall main idea.

In the lessons that follow, we will examine these elements of a well-organized piece of informative writing:

1. **Thesis**   In an informative piece of nonfiction writing, a writer usually presents one overall main idea. That main idea, or thesis, may be directly stated in the selection, or it may only be implied.

2. **Main Ideas**   Writers of nonfiction organize their writing by planning the main ideas they wish to present. Each of these main ideas supports or expands the overall main idea of the selection in some specific way.

3. **Supporting Details**   Good writers develop the main idea of a paragraph or passage by providing interesting facts and details.

LESSON 1

THESIS

The thesis of a piece of informative writing is the main idea that the author is trying to make about the subject of his or her writing. The writer often states the thesis in one or two sentences in the first paragraph. Many writers, however, prefer to use the opening paragraph or paragraphs to catch the readers' attention and interest. In that case the thesis statement may not appear until the second or third paragraph or later. It may not even appear until the last paragraph. Sometimes a writer repeats or restates this thesis two or three times. The repetition helps to connect the ideas in the selection. A restatement of the thesis at the end of an informative nonfiction selection can sometimes be an effective way to conclude the writing.

Reread the first section of "Pompeii: a Snapshot in Time," up to the subhead A Roman City. In this section Silverberg gives a brief preview of what follows in detail in the rest of the selection. He begins by trying to capture our attention and interest with a short, dramatic story of the eruption of Mount Vesuvius and the terrible rain of ashes that quickly buried Pompeii. He also wants to tell briefly what archaeologists have since uncovered in the buried city. Once he's captured our attention and interest, he can reveal the thesis of his informative selection.

Read this passage from the selection that comes near the end of the first section.

Not so with Pompeii. It was engulfed in an instant, and its people's tragedy was our great gain. The buildings of Pompeii still stand as they stood 2,000 years ago, and within the houses we can still see the pots and pans, the household tools, the hammers and nails. On the walls of the buildings are election slogans and the scrawlings of unruly boys. Pompeii is like a photograph in three dimensions. It shows us exactly what a city of the Roman Empire was like, down to the smallest detail of everyday life.

The last two sentences of this paragraph state the theis of the selection: "Pompeii is like a photograph in three dimensions. It shows us exactly what a city of the Roman Empire was like, down to the smallest detail of everyday life."

Silverberg's thesis is that the eruption of Mount Vesuvius froze everything in Pompeii at one moment in time, just as a photograph does. In the rest of the selection, he describes how this happened and what we can now see in Pompeii—a city preserved just as it was nearly 2,000 years ago by the volcanic ashes that covered it.

EXERCISE 1

Read this passage that comes at the end of the selection. Use what you have learned in this lesson to answer the questions that follow.

To enter Pompeii is to step into the Rome of the Caesars. An entire city, forever frozen in the last moment of its life by a terrible cataclysm, awaits the visitor. Thanks to the painstaking work of generations of devoted Italian archaeologists, we can experience today the most minute details of life 20 centuries ago in a Roman city. So much do we know of the people of Pompeii that they take on vivid life for us—the banker Jucundus, the wool merchant Vesonius, the newlywed Claudius Elogus, the nobleman Diomedes. The dreadful eruption that snatched the life of these people and this city in a single day also gave it a kind of immortality. Pompeii and its people live on today, in timeless permanence, their city transformed by Vesuvius' fury into a miraculous survivor of the ancient world.

1. You have learned that writers sometimes repeat or restate their thesis at the end of the selection. What sentence in this passage restates Silverberg's thesis?

2. How does that sentence express the same idea as Silverberg's thesis statement: "Pompeii is like a photograph in three dimensions. It shows us exactly what a city of the Roman Empire was like, down to the smallest detail of everyday life"?

Now check your answers with your teacher. Review this lesson if you don't understand why an answer was incorrect.

 WRITING ON YOUR OWN

In this exercise you will use what you have learned in this lesson to write a main-idea statement for your informative article. Follow these steps:

• Review the list of possible places you made for Writing: Developing an Informative Article. Choose one of these familiar places to be the subject of your article.
• Close your eyes and visualize yourself in this place. Imagine that you are doing something you usually do when you are there. Recall your thoughts and feelings about the place. Perhaps the place you have chosen is the workshop in the basement of your grandfather's house. In that case, think about what you do in the workshop and how you feel while you are working there.
• Make a list of words, phrases, or sentences that describe your thoughts and feelings. Do you feel calm and relaxed? Do you feel happy or sad? Do you feel energized, enthusiastic? Do you feel challenged? Do you feel creative?
• Use this list to create a thesis statement of one or two sentences for the informative article you are going to write. If you were writing about your grandfather's workshop, for example, your thesis might be "Grandfather's workshop is a place where I feel very safe and secure."

LESSON ② MAIN IDEAS

In informative nonfiction selections each paragraph or passage is organized around a main idea. These main ideas develop and explain the thesis of the article.

To develop and explain the thesis of his selection, Silverberg tells *how* Pompeii was destroyed and *how* archaeologists have been able to learn so much about the daily life of the people of ancient Pompeii. Each of these two main ideas plays an important part in supporting the thesis statement of the selection.

Read this passage from the first section of the selection.

The tragedy struck on the 24th of August, A.D. 79. Mount Vesuvius, which had slumbered quietly for centuries, exploded with savage violence. Death struck on a hot summer afternoon. Tons of hot ashes fell on Pompeii, smothering it, hiding it from sight. For three days the sun did not break through the cloud of volcanic ash that filled the sky. And when the eruption ended, Pompeii was buried deep. A thriving city had perished in a single day.

Centuries passed . . . Pompeii was forgotten. Then, 1,500 years later, it was discovered again. Beneath the protecting shroud of ashes, the city lay intact. Everything was as it had been the day Vesuvius erupted. There were still loaves of bread in the ovens of the bakeries. In the wine shops, the wine jars were in place, and on one counter could be seen a stain where a customer had thrown down his glass and fled.

In this excerpt Silverberg expresses two main ideas that supports the thesis statement. Look at the underlined sentences in those two paragraphs. The main idea of the first paragraph tells *how* the city was buried—Vesuvius exploded. The main idea of the second paragraph tells *how* archaeologists were able to learn about the details of daily life in Pompeii—the ashes covering the city preserved it and kept it intact. These two main ideas support Silverberg's thesis statement: "Pompeii is like a photograph in three dimensions. It shows us exactly what a city of the Roman Empire was like, down to the smallest detail of everyday life."

EXERCISE ②

Read this passage from the selection. Use what you have learned in this lesson to answer the questions that follow it.

> One of the truly fascinating aspects of Pompeii is the multitude of scribbled street signs. Notices were painted directly on the stone and have come down to us. At the big ampitheater, an inscription tells us, "The troupe of gladiators owned by Suettius Centus will give a performance at Pompeii on May 31st. There will be an animal show. The awnings will be used." And at the theater where plays were given, a message to a popular actor reads, "Actius, beloved of the people, come back soon; fare thee well!"

1. Which sentence states the main idea of this paragraph?

2. How does this main idea relate to the thesis of the selection?

Now check your answers with your teacher. Review this part of the lesson if you don't understand why an answer was incorrect.

WRITING ON YOUR OWN ②

In this exercise you will use what you learned in this lesson to develop several main ideas for your article.

- Reread the thesis statement that you wrote for Writing on Your Own 1. Your statement expresses the general feelings you associate with the place you are going to write about. Make a graphic organizer like the one that follows and write in your thesis statement.

Thesis Statement

Main Ideas

Supporting Details | (facts, examples, anecdotes)

- Now ask yourself what these feelings are based on. Why does this place cause these feelings in you? If you were writing about your grandfather's workshop, you would explain *why* you feel secure there.
- Each reason you give for why you feel the way you do about this place is a main idea. Write your main ideas in the graphic organizer. For example, if you were writing about your grandfather's workshop, you might write these two main ideas: "Everything is in its proper place" and "There are rules for everything."
- Save your graphic organizer to use again later in this unit.

LESSON 3   SUPPORTING DETAILS

Main ideas are not very meaningful unless they are supported with details. Silverberg uses several kinds of supporting details to give meaning and interest to the selection's main ideas.

One kind of supporting detail is facts. A *fact* is something known to be true or to have really happened. In "Pompeii: A Snapshot in Time," Silverberg uses many facts, such as dates, measurements, peoples' names, and names of objects found in the ruins. Read this passage to see how the author uses facts to support the paragraph's main idea.

> Until that year Pompeii was a prosperous city of 25,000 people. Nearby was the Bay of Naples, an arm of the blue Mediterranean. Rich men came down from wealthy Rome, 125 miles to the north, to build luxurious seaside villas. Fertile farmlands occupied the fields surrounding Pompeii. Rising sharply behind the city was the 4,000-foot bulk of Mount Vesuvius, a grass-covered slope where the shepherds of Pompeii took their goats to graze. Pompeii was a busy city and a happy one.

The first sentence of the paragraph states the main idea—Pompeii was a prosperous city of 25,000 people. The following facts are details that support that main idea: (1) rich men came from Rome to build luxurious seaside villas; (2) fertile farmlands surrounded Pompeii; (3) Pompeii was a busy city and a happy one.

Facts also include statements by other people. Silverberg quotes the Roman philosopher Pliny, an eyewitness to the eruption of Mount Vesuvius. He reported that the cloud of ash and dirt from the volcano was shaped like a pine tree. Pliny's description helps the reader picture the great ashen cloud over Pompeii on that day.

A second type of supporting detail that Silverberg uses is examples. An *example* explains or specifically illustrates a general statement. In the part of the selection following the subhead *The Last Day*, Silverberg gives examples that show how normal life was on the morning of the eruption: the rumble of the carts entering the city, the busy shops, children heading to school, a boy scribbling on a wall, and men discussing business. These examples support Silverberg's statements: "The quiet morning moved slowly along. There was nothing very unusual about Pompeii. Hundreds of other towns just like it dotted the rolling plains of Italy."

Anecdotes are a third type of supporting detail used by writers. An *anecdote* is a short account of some interesting incident or event. Like a short story, an anecdote has characters, a setting, and a plot. Writers use anecdotes to support their opinions and to add interest to their writing.

As you read the following anecdote, think about why Silverberg has chosen it. How does this anecdote support his main idea?

> In those first few hours, only the quick-witted managed to escape. Vesonius Primus, the wealthy wool merchant, called his family together and piled jewelry and money into a sack. Lighting a torch, Vesonius led his little band out into the nightmare of the streets. Overlooked in the confusion was Vesonius' black watchdog, chained in the courtyard. The terrified dog barked wildly as lapilli struck and drifting white ash settled around him. The animal struggled with his chain, battling fiercely to get free, but the chain held, and no one heard the dog's cries. The humans were too busy saving themselves.

This anecdote serves several purposes. First, it reveals two human reactions to the life-threatening situation. Vesonius Primus was caring for his family *and* he was being practical by saving his jewelry and money. By telling you that Vesonius had to light a torch in the middle of the day, Silverberg is giving you an idea of how dark the city had become even though it was early afternoon. The details about Versonius's dog

emphasize the fact that even those who escaped the city suffered. They left behind many things they cared about and
loved. Finally, the anecdote emphasizes that the remarkably
well-preserved remains found in the city—including the
unfortunate dog—have enabled archaeologists to reconstruct
many of the events of that day. The anecdote supports the
selection's main idea by describing some of the smallest
details of life in Pompeii on that deadly day.

EXERCISE ③

Read this passage from the selection. Use what you have
learned in this lesson to answer the questions that follow it.

> The rich man Diomedes was another of those who
> decided not to flee at the first sign of alarm. Rather
> than risk being crushed by the screaming mobs,
> Diomedes calmly led the members of his household into
> the solidly built basement of his villa. Sixteen people
> altogether, as well as his daughter's dog and her beloved
> little goat. They took enough food and water to last for
> several days.
>
> But for all his shrewdness and foresight, Diomedes
> was undone anyway. Poison gas was creeping slowly
> into the underground shelter! He watched his daugh-
> ter begin to cough and struggle for breath. Vesuvius
> was giving off vast quantities of deadly carbon monox-
> ide that was now settling like a blanket over the dying
> city. . . .

1. What type of supporting detail is used in the above passage?
   Explain the reason for your choice.

2. How does this type of detail help to support the main idea of
   the selection?

Now check your answers with your teacher. Review this lesson if you don't understand why an answer was incorrect.

WRITING ON YOUR OWN ③

In this exercise you will use what you learned in this lesson to add supporting details to your graphic organizer. Follow these steps:

- Look at the main ideas you wrote in your graphic organizer for Writing on Your Own 2. Now you will add details that support those secondary ideas.
- Think about the three kinds of supporting details you learned about in this lesson. Try to think of several facts, examples, and at least one anecdote to add to your organizer. Write them in the organizer.

DISCUSSION GUIDES

1. Silverberg says that some Pompeiians fled the city to safety when Vesuvius erupted, while others remained in the city. In a small group discuss why you think many of the people stayed in the city. You may use examples from the selection to support your opinions. Share your observations with the rest of the class.

2. In a small group discuss the following: Imagine that your city or town was buried and preserved for nearly two thousand years, just as Pompeii was. What evidence would future archaeologists find that would show that daily life in your time was *like* daily life in ancient Pompeii? What evidence would show that daily life today was *different* from that in Pompeii nearly two thousand years ago?

3. Besides giving you ideas and facts you did not know before, "Pompeii: A Snapshot in Time" may have raised some questions in your mind. For example, you may be curious about how Pompeii came to be rediscovered or if Mount Vesuvius has ever erupted again. Skim the selection and write down any questions you may have. Share your questions with the class and discuss how or where you might find answers. Have volunteers do research to find the answers and present them to the rest of the class.

WRITE AN INFORMATIVE ARTICLE

In this unit you have learned how to use main ideas and sup-porting details to develop an informative article about a favorite familiar place.

Follow these steps to complete your informative article. If you have any questions about the writing process, refer to Using the Writing Process (page 220).

- Gather and review the following pieces of writing you did in this unit: 1) a list of familiar places and details about each, 2) your thesis statement, 3) the graphic organizer to which you added main ideas and supporting details to your thesis statement.
- Using the information from your graphic organizer, write an introductory paragraph identifying and describing the place you've chosen for the subject of your article. Decide whether to include your thesis statement in this opening paragraph or to use it in a later paragraph. Remember that you want to attract your reader's attention and interest in the opening paragraph, so make your description vivid and interesting.
- Add two or more paragraphs to complete your article. Include your thesis statement if you did not include it in the opening paragraph. Use the details from your organizer to support and expand on your main ideas. Be sure to explain why the place you've chosen means so much to you.
- With a classmate, exchange finished articles. After reading, critique each other's work and make suggestions for improvements. If any suggested changes seem warranted, revise your article accordingly.
- Proofread your final draft for errors in spelling, grammar, punctuation, and capitalization. Make a final copy and save it in your writing portfolio.

How a Biographer Interprets Facts

The Soul Selects Her Own Society

Excerpt from *I'm Nobody! Who Are You? The Story of Emily Dickinson* by Edna Barth

INTRODUCTION

BUILDING BACKGROUND

Emily Dickinson is recognized as one of the best American poets of the 19th century. She observed life closely and used her poetry to explore questions about love, death, faith, and nature. Dickinson's verses are quite unlike any poet's before or after her. She believed strongly in the power of words. To Dickinson, words themselves seemed alive:

> A word is dead
> When it is said,
> Some say.
> I say it just
> Begins to live
> That day.

This image of Emily Dickinson is a detail from a portrait of the Dickinson children painted by O. A. Bullard in 1840. Emily would have been about 10 years old at the time.

Dickinson's poetry was unusual for the times. She used dashes frequently in her verse. Like a rest mark in music, the dash indicates a pause. She also capitalized the first letters of words as a way to add emphasis, and she didn't always use exact rhyme. As a poet, Dickinson sought to create the most meaning and greatest feeling in the fewest words possible. Most of her poems are less than 20 lines long.

Dickinson was born in Amherst, Massachusetts, on December 10, 1830. She had an older brother, Austin, and a younger sister, Lavinia (Vinnie). Her father, a successful lawyer, was one of the wealthiest men in Amherst. The Dickinsons lived a very comfortable, upper-class life.

Even though Dickinson had a limited social life and rarely left home, she was a very well-educated woman for her time. She attended Amherst Academy and then Mount Holyoke Female Seminary, a college for women. More importantly, Dickinson was very well read. She was well acquainted with the classics and with the works of important writers of her own time.

As Dickinson grew older, she spent less and less time socializing and more and more time with her family or by herself. During the last several decades of her life, she became a recluse, seldom leaving her home.

No one will ever really know what led Dickinson to live such a secluded life. Many readers think that her heart had been broken by a failed love affair. It seems just as likely, however, that Emily had never met anyone who truly understood her. She met few people who thought or felt as deeply about life as she did.

In spite of her uneventful life and limited experiences, Dickinson was a very intense and emotional person. She looked very closely at what she saw, and she put her thoughts into her poems. She called her poems "my letter to the World / That never wrote to Me—."

ABOUT THE AUTHOR

Edna Barth is the author of 16 nonfiction books on various subjects. Her first job was as a librarian. Later, she worked as an editor for several New York publishing companies.

Barth said that she had never considered writing about Emily Dickinson until she took her first job in the public library in Amherst, Massachusetts, Dickinson's hometown. The more she learned about the town's famous former resident, the more curious she became to know and understand this gifted poet. Most of what Barth learned about the poet and her life came from Dickinson's poems and letters, the letters others wrote to her, and the written memories of a few friends and family members. From these materials, Barth wrote *I'm Nobody! Who Are You? The Story of Emily Dickinson*—a woman and a poet "who, above all, never tried to be anything but herself." Edna Barth died in 1980.

ABOUT THE LESSONS	The lessons that follow "The Soul Selects Her Own Society" focus on how a biographer selects and interprets facts.

You will learn how Edna Barth has chosen facts and how she interprets the life of Dickinson. Like most biographers Barth has carefully chosen which information she will include about her subject. By choosing certain facts and leaving out others, Barth gives her own interpretation, or view, of what Emily Dickinson was like.

WRITING: DEVELOPING A BIOGRAPHICAL SKETCH

At the end of this unit you will write a biographical sketch. A *biographical sketch* is a brief story about a real person. The suggestions that follow will help you get started:

- Think about a person in your family who is special to you—one of your grandparents, your mother or father, a brother or a sister, or even a cousin, an aunt, or an uncle, perhaps.
- Does the person have a talent that you think is special? Does he or she have a job you find particularly interesting? Why is this person so special to you?

- Write down the name of the family member whom you want to write about. Then make a few notes about why this person is special to you.

| AS YOU READ | Think about these questions as you read "The Soul Selects Her Own Society." They will help you identify Barth's interpretation of Dickinson's life. |

- What is the theme—the underlying message, or central idea—in Barth's biography?
- What facts about Dickinson's life does Barth use to support her theme?
- What do you think is the author's opinion of Dickinson as a person and as a poet? How can you tell?

The Soul Selects Her Own Society

Excerpt from *I'm Nobody! Who Are You? The Story of Emily Dickinson* by Edna Barth

Emily could bake a loaf of rye and Indian bread that brought a gleam of pleasure to her father's eye. He refused to eat bread baked by any other hand. She could darn a sock so skillfully that he couldn't say where the hole had been. He enjoyed having Emily cater[1] to him, an excuse she gave for not leaving home.

One of her greatest pleasures was her flower garden, where wildflowers bloomed as well as roses, lilies, and jasmine. But for the deepest satisfaction she turned inward to the world of her imagination.

> *To make a prairie it takes a clover and one bee*
> *One clover, and a bee,*
> *And revery.[2]*
> *The revery alone will do,*
> *If bees are few.*

The hours for writing were too few. Church services, club meetings, and gossiping neighbors took up time. Emily pre-

---

[1] to provide anything needed or wished for

[2] daydreaming; a thoughtful state

ferred a few people she could feel really close to, though even these she seldom saw. A large part of any friendship was carried on by means of notes, sent sometimes with a jar of jelly, some choice apples, or a flower. "The Soul selects her own Society—" she wrote in one of her poems, "Then—shuts the Door—"

The family had come to accept Emily's ways, but Austin and her father became annoyed at times when she refused to see a family friend.

Vinnie indulged Emily in her ways, willingly answering the doorbell, or delivering notes and flowers for her. With a flash of her dark eyes she quickly disposed of prying questions. "Why didn't Emily go to the sewing circle like everybody else?" "Why should she?" was Vinnie's retort. "If she's more contented to stay at home?"

Austin's marriage was not turning out as the family had hoped. His beautiful Sue was more self-centered than any of them had guessed. Being the wife of young Squire Dickinson seemed more important to her than Austin himself. The Dickinsons in the brick house next door shook their heads over the amounts of money she spent. Sue was never happier than when the driveway of the Evergreens[3] was crowded with the carriages of guests, and the whole house ablaze with lights.

"Glitter," Emily summed it up.

Sue could be cutting and often hurt Emily, but Emily usually forgave her and, in spite of everything, went on admiring her and sending her poems.

Sue and Austin had no son to carry on the family name, or any children at all as yet. Emily knew how this must prey upon Austin, and anything that troubled Austin troubled her.

Sometime in 1860, the year she was thirty years old, Emily fell in love, though who the man was no one has ever been sure. Some of the people who have studied her poems and let-

---

[3] the large house Mr. Dickinson built next to his own for Austin and Sue

ters think it was Charles Wadsworth,[4] and others, Samuel Bowles.[5] A man she called "Master" had begun appearing in letters and poems.

By now she had copied 150 poems into the little booklets. She had written about friendship, about life and death, about coming to know one's self. Now the poems were centering on love.

"'Tis so much joy! 'Tis so much joy!" one of the poems begins, and another, "Come slowly, Eden!" There were also poems in which she saw herself dressed in white or used the word *wife*, as if she considered herself married in spirit.

Then, within the year, Emily found out that the man she loved did not love her.

From almost delirious joy she plunged into deepest despair. For months afterward, in handwriting as chaotic as her state of mind, she poured her emotions into her writing. Poems such as "I felt a Funeral, in my Brain" show how over-whelmed she felt, and in some of her letters there are hints that she even feared losing her mind. No poem or letter was dated, but handwriting experts have guessed at the dates by a study of the changing script.

More and more of her words began with capital letters, and more were underlined. She used dashes more freely than ever, giving a breathless effect.

One poem written during the crisis struck a different, more optimistic note:

> "Hope" is the thing with feathers—
> That perches in the soul—
> And sings the tune without the words—
> And never stops—at all—
>
> (first stanza)

---

[4] a Presbyterian minister with whom Emily corresponded for many years

[5] editor of the *Springfield Republican*

The Republican Abraham Lincoln had been elected president on a platform[6] calling for the end of slavery in the United States territories. He took office as the Confederates fired on the Union ship *Star of the West* at Fort Sumter, South Carolina. The Civil War had begun.

Southern students at Amherst College left in a body. Northern students and young men of the town rushed to enlist in the Union army. Soon there were Amherst people receiving reports of their sons' deaths.

The war reached Emily obliquely. No one in her family fought. For months she had suffered from a strange sense of terror. Her writing gave her something solid to lean on.

In May 1861, one of her poems appeared, unsigned, in the *Springfield Republican*. It begins like this:

I taste a liquor never brewed—
From Tankards scooped in Pearl—

In June a son, Edward Dickinson, was born to Austin and Sue, a frail, sickly child who kept his mother preoccupied.[7] Sue had little time to think of poetry these days. She and Emily had drawn somewhat apart. Yet Emily went on sending her poems. Two years before, she had written a poem that is now famous: "Safe in their Alabaster[8] Chambers." The second stanza was not to Sue's liking, and Emily had written a new one. When Sue told her it didn't go with the ghostly shimmer of the first stanza, Emily wrote another. "Is this frostier?" she asked. Sue could tell her, she hinted, if only she would be sincere. Then she admitted that her greatest ambition was someday to make Sue and Austin proud of her.

Austin seemed out of sorts. The birth of a son had done nothing to bring him any closer to his wife. Mother was com-

---

[6] a formal, written declaration of principles by a group or political party

[7] lost in thought; distracted; deeply concerned about something

[8] a smooth, bright white mineral

plaining of neuralgia,[9] and Father was irritable. "Such a family!" Vinnie said. "I really despair of you all." She herself had taken to adopting cats. Emily had always looked forward to March, but this year she hardly noticed.

One blustery day Vinnie was out at the clotheslines energetically beating rugs, long past the time she usually went to the post office for the mail. Now she came into the house, her cheeks rosy, bringing with her a rush of tingling air.

"Can't you go now?" Emily begged, hoping desperately for letters from the few friends who were so important to her.

There were no letters that day, but in the Original Poetry column in the *Springfield Republican* was her poem "Safe in their Alabaster Chambers." In bitter disappointment she stared at the lines she had written and rewritten so many times. The editors had changed some of the words. It was no longer her poem. She was glad she had not signed her name.

On his doctor's advice, Samuel Bowles, who had developed heart trouble, was going to Europe, a whole ocean away. Charles Wadsworth, meanwhile, had been called to a church in San Francisco, a whole continent away.

Emily felt abandoned. More desperately than ever she turned to her poetry. At times she knew with deep certainty that it was good. With this came the feeling that life was good too.

At other times doubt crept in. Who said that her work was good? She herself, a few friends, a few editors. Editors distorted her verses for the sake of mere rhyme. Friends sometimes hinted that her poems, while remarkable, were strange "airy" things, not rooted enough in earth.

Perhaps she was no poet at all. Dark overwhelming forces seemed to rush toward her at the thought.

As if in answer, the *Atlantic Monthly* for April 1862 ran the article "Letter to a Young Contributor." The author was Thomas Wentworth Higginson, whose books Emily knew and

---

[9] pain, usually sharp, along the course of a nerve

liked. In his article, he wrote as if directly to her. He urged young writers to charge their style with life, and to work and rework. No word that could be done without should be left in. One word could express volumes, and half a sentence a whole lifetime. "Literature is attar[10] of roses," he wrote. "One distilled drop from a million blossoms."

Higginson spoke of the mystery and majesty of words and the importance of the poet's calling. In the flowery language of the time, he said what Emily herself believed.

She read on to the end, then went back to reread the words "charge your style with life."

Surely the man who had written this could tell her what she wanted to know about her own writing. Emily sat down at the first opportunity with pen and notepaper.

Barefoot Rank

A few days later in Worcester, Massachusetts, Thomas Wentworth Higginson opened Emily's letter.

"Mr. Higginson," he read, "are you too deeply occupied to say if my verse is alive?" She was not sure herself, she explained, and had no one to ask. At the end she urged him to keep the whole thing a secret. There was no signature on the letter. As if hiding from view, Emily had written her name on a card tucked into a smaller envelope.

With her letter were four poems, without titles, like all her others. "Safe in their Alabaster Chambers" was one. Another was a poem which, today, is a great favorite. It begins:

I'll tell you how the Sun rose—
A Ribbon at a time—

In his "Letter to a Young Contributor," Mr. Higginson had urged that dashes be used very sparingly. This young contribu-

---

[10] a fragrant oil made from distilled flower petals

tor had filled her poems with dashes. Many of the nouns began with capital letters—a style no longer in fashion. Worse still, the young lady seemed to know nothing of rhyme or even grammar and spelling. There were flashes of something new and original in her verses, but in his opinion she had a long way to go if she ever hoped to become a poet.

Thomas Wentworth Higginson was a Unitarian minister who had left the pulpit to write and lecture on such subjects as the abolition of slavery and women's rights. As an ex-minister, he was used to having people lean on him. He would do what he could to help poor Miss Dickinson.

Emily read Mr. Higginson's reply with a mixture of excitement and disappointment. Though he praised the originality of her poems, it was clear that he didn't know what to make of them.

One of the poems was "We play at Paste—till qualified for Pearl." By including it, Emily hinted that she was no longer a beginner, but a poet, eager to perfect her art. Mr. Higginson, it was clear, thought otherwise. He urged her to master grammar, improve her rhyme, and try for smoother, more flowing lines.

Emily read the letter again. At least Mr. Higginson took her seriously. And she warmed to the kindness and sympathy between the lines.

Ten days later she sent off another note and three more poems.

Mr. Higginson had asked her age, and she answered by saying, "I made no verse but one or two until—this winter—sir—"

Then she confessed, "I had a terror—since September—I could tell to none—and so I sing, as the Boy does by the Burying Ground—because I am afraid—"

She answered the questions about her favorite books and about her friends. Ben Newton[11] was the friend who had

---

[11] a young man Emily met when he was a clerk in her father's law office; one of Emily's closest male friends when she was young (They had long, serious conversations about religion, life, death, and immortality; he died while still very young.)

taught her Immortality. "But venturing too close himself, he never returned," she said.

Samuel Bowles, the other friend she mentioned, "was not content I should be his scholar—so he left the land."

Her companions? "Hills—sir—and the Sundown—and a Dog—as large as myself that my Father bought me —They are better than Beings—because they know—but do not tell—"

"I have a brother and sister—my mother does not care for thought—and a father, too busy with his briefs—to notice what we do—"

She was thirty-one years old, but spoke of herself, her brother, and sister as children.

She begged her new teacher to tell her how to become a poet. In the same sentence she suggested that perhaps, like melody or witchcraft, it could not be taught.

Among the poems enclosed with this second letter was one meant to be sent to a friend, with a flower:

> *South Winds jostle them—*
> *Bumblebees come—*
> *Hover—hesitate—*
> *Drink, and are gone—*
>
> *Butterflies pause*
> *On their passage Cashmere—*
> *I—softly plucking,*
> *Present them here!*

Another was a beautiful poem with the following first stanza:

> *Of all the Sounds despatched abroad,*
> *There's not a Charge to me*
> *Like that old measure in the Boughs—*
> *That phraseless Melody—*
> *The Wind does—working like a Hand,*

Whose fingers Comb the Sky—
Then quiver down—with tufts of Tune—
Permitted Gods, and me—

The third was a love poem of seven stanzas, the first of which appears below:

There came a Day at Summer's full,
Entirely for me—
I thought that such were for the Saints,
Where Resurrections—be—

This time, feeling bolder, Emily signed the letter, "Your friend, E. Dickinson."

The three poems brought more praise than the first set, as well as further criticism.

"I have had few pleasures as deep as your opinion," Emily wrote back, and in the same letter, "My dying Tutor told me that he would like to live till I had been a poet . . ."

Since she seemed to have trouble rhyming properly, Mr. Higginson had said, perhaps she should drop rhyme altogether. But Emily explained that she "could not drop the Bells whose jingling cooled my Tramp."

In most poetry of the time, lines ended in exact rhymes. Many of Emily's poems were rhymed in this way. But when it suited her purpose, she used other, more subtle kinds. One of these was *suspended rhyme*, in which different vowel sounds are followed by the same consonant:

human

common

Another was *imperfect rhyme*. Here, two rhyming words end with the same vowel sound, followed by different consonants:

field

steal

Mr. Higginson had advised Emily to be in no hurry to publish her poems. This made her smile. Nothing was further from her mind, she assured him. "If fame belonged to me, I could not escape her—if she did not, the longest day would pass me on the chase . . . My Barefoot—Rank is better—"

In her heart Emily knew that Thomas Higginson would never be the critic and teacher she had hoped for. But she was grateful for any comment from the man who had written as he had in the *Atlantic Monthly* about the importance of the poet's calling.

Her solitary life dismayed him, and he urged her to mingle more. Emily wrote back, shyly asking if he would have time to be the friend he felt she needed.

More curious than ever, Mr. Higginson asked her to send a picture of herself.

Instead, there came this description: "I had no portrait now, but I am small, like the Wren, and my Hair is bold, like the Chestnut Bur—and my eyes like the sherry the guest leaves in the glass."

In August Mr. Higginson's letters stopped coming. Autumn arrived. Apples ripened in the orchard, Concord grapes hung in heavy blue clusters, and the walnuts and hazelnuts were brown.

With her dog at her side, Emily walked through the crackling leaves, filling her basket. It soothed her and cleared her mind. "But why don't I have a letter from Mr. Higginson?" she said to Carlo. "Have I displeased him?" That evening she wrote and asked.

Thomas Higginson had been drilling a company of Massachusetts soldiers. In November he took over leadership of the first official regiment of ex-slaves in the Union army. Occupied as he was, Thomas Higginson, now a colonel, took time to write to her from an army camp.

At last the war was touching Emily more directly. Fearful that she might lose her new friend, she wrote back, "I should have liked to see you before you became improbable."

Samuel Bowles had returned from Europe, and Emily

wrote to him at once. As she had so many times before, she told him how much she thought of him. And she begged him not to start working again until he was really well.

Only a few days later, he came to Amherst, and the Dickinsons were delighted. Samuel Bowles was a favorite with all of them.

"Come down, Emily. Sam's here," Austin called from the foot of the stairs.

There was no answer. At the sound of Samuel Bowles's deep-throated laugh, Emily was too overcome with emotion. When Vinnie came looking for her, she gave her a little note for him.

This, after the devotion-filled letters Emily had been writing! Samuel Bowles felt snubbed but, in his lighthearted way, he made a joke of it, sending his regards to the "Queen Recluse" in a letter to Austin. In another he sent Emily a message, chiding her for ignoring him.

Emily meanwhile had given up colored dresses, wearing only white, a symbol, apparently, that she was dedicating her life to someone or something.

I'm Nobody! Who Are You?

People found her poetry puzzling. Editors and critics like Samuel Bowles, Dr. Holland, and Thomas Higginson thought most of it unsuitable to print. Emily was becoming resigned to this.

Far from being discouraged, she was writing one poem after another. In 1862 alone, she wrote 365, among them the one beginning:

> This is my letter to the World
> That never wrote to Me—

If her poems were published at all, she would remain anonymous. There would be no froglike croaking of her own name.

I'm nobody! Who are you?
Are you—Nobody—too?
Then there's a pair of us?
Don't tell! They'd advertise—you know!

How dreary—to be—Somebody!
How public—like a Frog—
To tell one's name—the livelong June—
To an admiring Bog!

During 1863, still distraught,[12] Emily went on writing. That year there were about 140 poems she considered good enough to join the others tucked away in her bottom bureau drawer.

Though she knew now that Thomas Higginson could teach her little, she went on pretending to be his student. About a year before, she had complained in one of her poems of being "shut up in prose" just as she had been shut in a closet, as a child—to keep her still.

Here was another who wanted to shut Emily up in prose. Nevertheless, she considered Thomas Higginson her friend.

Most of Emily's letters that year went to her cousins, Louisa and Fanny Norcross in Boston, who had just lost their father. Louisa was now twenty-one and Fanny sixteen, but Emily continued to speak as if she and they were small children.

"Fanny and Loo are such geese," Vinnie said, and no one else gave them credit for great intelligence. But Emily had taken them to her heart, and loved them as they were. With them she shared some of her troubles as well as details of her daily life omitted from letters to others.

In February and again in April she went to Boston to see an eye doctor, staying with her cousins. They were kind to her, but she found being away from home more painful than

---

[12] anxious; upset

the eye ailment. She would be willing to *walk* to Amherst, she wrote to Vinnie, sleeping in the bushes along the way.

One January day in 1866 when Amherst was buried in snow, Carlo died. Emily was heartbroken. She had lost her "shaggy ally," as she called him. No other dog could ever replace him.

About a month afterward, Emily opened the *Springfield Republican* to find a poem about a snake she had written the year before. It began:

> A *narrow Fellow in the Grass*
> *Occasionally rides—*

The meaning of the third and fourth lines had been altered by a change in her punctuation. Editors!

And who had given them the poem? Sue, of course. For years now Sue had been ambitious for her protégé.[13] "We must launch you," she often said.

Emily was hurt and angry. What would Thomas Higginson think of this? She had told him that she did not "print." Now she would have to apologize. Not to publish had become a point of honor with her.

For the next few years Emily went on writing but more slowly. Her letters to Thomas Higginson were fewer. When she did write, he was slow in answering.

"Sometimes I take out your letters & verses," he explained once, "and when I feel their strange power, it is not strange that I find it hard to write & that long months pass. I have the greatest desire to see you, always feeling that perhaps if I could once take you by the hand I might be something to you; but till then you only enshroud[14] yourself in this fiery mist & I

---

[13] someone whose education or training is directed by an influential person

[14] to cover with a veil or shadow

cannot reach you, but only rejoice in the rare sparkles of light.

"It is hard for me to understand how you can live so alone, with thoughts of such a quality coming up in you & even the companionship of your dog withdrawn."

Then he asked her if she ever came to Boston. "All ladies do," he said, inviting her to a meeting of the Women's Club at which he would read a paper on the Greek goddesses.

Politely but firmly Emily refused. Her eye doctor did want her to return to Boston for a checkup, she admitted, but leaving home was impossible. Her father was too accustomed to having her nearby.

She urged Colonel Higginson to come to Amherst instead, explaining, "I do not cross my father's ground to any house or town."

REVIEWING AND INTERPRETING

Record your answers to these questions in your personal literature notebook. Follow the directions for each part.

REVIEWING   Try to complete each of these sentences without looking back at the selection.

Recalling Facts

1. Thomas Wentworth Higginson was
   a. Dickinson's publisher.
   b. the pastor of Emily's church.
   c. a writer and lecturer.
   d. a Dickinson family friend.

Understanding Main Ideas

2. Dickinson's sister, Vinnie,
   a. read and criticized Emily's poems.
   b. supported Emily despite her shy ways.
   c. envied her sister-in-law Sue.
   d. was annoyed when Dickinson refused to see guests.

Identifying Sequence

3. Dickinson began writing to Higginson
   a. while she was a child.
   b. before the Civil War began.
   c. during the Civil War.
   d. following the death of her parents.

Finding Supporting Details

4. Dickinson showed her trust in Higginson by
   a. signing her name to her second letter.
   b. following his advice about improving her poetry.
   c. pretending to be his student.
   d. visiting him when she was in Boston.

Getting Meaning from Context

5. "The war reached Emily obliquely. No one in her family fought." The word *obliquely* means
   a. painfully.
   b. indirectly.
   c. deeply.
   d. slowly.

INTERPRETING To complete these items, you may look back at the selection if you'd like.

Making Inferences

6. From this selection, it is clear that
   a. few people knew Dickinson well.
   b. Dickinson's family discouraged her from writing poetry.
   c. Dickinson's family encouraged her to write poetry.
   d. Dickinson was poorly educated.

Generalizing

7. Emily's sister, Vinnie,
   a. recognized Dickinson's talent.
   b. envied Dickinson's talent.
   c. protected and defended Dickinson.
   d. disagreed often with her parents.

Recognizing Fact and Opinion

8. Which of the following is a statement of opinion?
   a. "She was thirty-one years old, but spoke of herself, her brother, and sister as children."
   b. "I have a brother and sister—my mother does not care for thought—and a father, too busy with his briefs—to notice what we do—"
   c. "People found her poetry puzzling."
   d. "For years now Sue had been ambitious for her protégé."

Identifying Cause and Effect

9. Emily continued to correspond with Higginson because she
   a. felt she could learn from him.
   b. valued his opinion.
   c. hoped he would publish her poems.
   d. was grateful for his attention.

Drawing Conclusions **10.** From what you have learned about Dickinson in this selection, you can conclude that

a. she was ashamed of her appearance.

b. she knew her poems would be published after her death.

c. she was treated unfairly by her family.

d. fame was not important to her.

Now check your answers with your teacher. Study the questions you answered incorrectly. What skills are they checking? Talk with your teacher about ways to work on those skills.

How a Biographer Interprets Facts

Biographies and autobiographies are among the most popular forms of nonfiction. A *biography* is the story of a real person's life written by someone else. An *autobiography* is the story of a real person's life written by that person. Both words come from the Greek roots *bio*, meaning "life" and *graph*, meaning "writing." The prefix *auto-* means "self." So *biography* means "life writing," and *autobiography* is "self-life writing." The *subject* of a biography or autobiography is the person whose life story is being told.

Why are biographies so popular? Readers are curious about people who have accomplished important deeds or have had interesting experiences. You may wonder what made a person so brave or how a person developed a certain talent. It's fascinating and exciting to find out what it felt like to be the first person to step onto the surface of the moon. It's also interesting to see how a biographer weaves those facts and details together to form an interpretation of the subject's character and the meaning of his or her life.

In this selection from *I'm Nobody! Who Are You? The True Story of Emily Dickinson,* you learned some facts about Dickinson's life and experiences. As you study the lessons in this unit, you will see how Barth interpreted these facts. An *interpretation* is one person's view of the meaning of certain words, events, or actions. Barth provides facts about Dickinson and about events that took place in her life. Barth then evaluates and interprets these events and tries to explain how they affected Dickinson. Biographers start with facts, but as you will learn, they must also use their imaginations to bring these facts to life and spark your interest.

Many elements must combine to make a good biography. In the lessons that follow, we will talk about three of those elements:

1. **Primary and Secondary Sources**   Before writing a biography, the author does thorough research into the subject's life. The biographer first looks for primary sources (information that comes directly from the time the subject lived) and secondary sources (information about the subject that came from a later time). The biographer then decides which sources are the most reliable and which facts to include in the biography.

2. **Interpretation and Theme**   Once the biographer decides which facts to include, he or she then establishes a *theme*—the underlying message, or central idea, that the writer wants to convey to the reader. The theme is built on the biographer's interpretation of the events and people in the subject's life.

3. **Biographer's Opinion**   The biographer expresses his or her opinion of the subject, and then organizes the facts and events of the subject's life to support that opinion.

LESSON ①   PRIMARY AND SECONDARY SOURCES

How does a biographer select the facts to use in a subject's biography? Whether the subject is living or not, a good biographer tries to investigate every aspect of that person's life. Sometimes a biographer interviews the subject and directly learns the facts and details that are known only by the subject.

But what if, as in Barth's case, the subject cannot be interviewed? Dickinson has been dead for more then a century. Barth recognized the need for a primary source of information. A *primary source* is information that comes directly from the subject's own experience or from material written about or to the subject during her or his lifetime. The most important reason for using primary sources in a biography is to create an accurate picture of the subject. Primary sources may include letters, speeches, diaries, or anything else written by or about the subject. To understand Dickinson, Barth wanted to read what the poet had written—her poems and letters.

To get a complete picture of Dickinson, Barth also had to use secondary sources. A *secondary source* is information that is written at a later time. For example, an encyclopedia article about Dickinson is a secondary source. In Barth's research primary sources include letters and other writings by Dickinson's friends and family, newspaper and magazine articles of the time, and public records. Her secondary sources include other biographies of Dickinson.

Even though primary and secondary sources about Dickinson's life are limited, Barth still had more information about her subject than she could possibly put into one book. In writing the biography, she had to select the facts that would best support her theme and her interpretation of Dickinson's life.

Read this passage from the selection and think about how the information that Barth has chosen helps her to create an accurate picture of Emily Dickinson's life for the reader.

> For the next few years Emily went on writing but more slowly. Her letters to Thomas Higginson were fewer. When she did write, he was slow in answering.
>
> "Sometimes I take out your letters & verses," he explained once, "and when I feel their strange power, it is not strange that I find it hard to write & that long months pass. I have the greatest desire to see you, always feeling that perhaps if I could once take you by the hand I might be something to you; but till then you only enshroud yourself in this fiery mist & I cannot reach you, but only rejoice in the rare sparkles of light.
>
> "It is hard for me to understand how you can live so alone, with thoughts of such a quality coming up in you & even the companionship of your dog withdrawn."
>
> Then he asked her if she ever came to Boston. "All ladies do," he said, inviting her to a meeting of the Women's Club at which he would read a paper on the Greek goddesses.

Politely but firmly Emily refused. Her eye doctor did want her to return to Boston for a checkup, she admitted, but leaving home was impossible. Her father was too accustomed to having her nearby.

She urged Colonel Higginson to come to Amherst instead, explaining, "I do not cross my father's ground to any house or town."

What have you learned from the first few sentences of this passage? First, the information is from a primary source. The author has compared the number of letters that Dickinson and Higginson used to exchange to the number of letters they later wrote to each other. By looking at the dates on the letters, Barth can see that they were not writing so frequently as they once had been. Now think about what is implied by this. Barth is showing that Dickinson and Higginson were finding it more and more difficult to communicate with each other. Dickinson's search for someone who could share her deepest thoughts and feelings had failed.

Barth has quoted sentences from several of Higginson's letters to show his thoughts and feelings during this period. He revealed that he thought about Dickinson more often than he wrote to her. By speaking of the "strange power" of her verses, he told her that he had come to realize that her poetry was important but that he still did not understand it. He said, "perhaps if I could take you by the hand I might be something to you." He thought that if he and Dickinson could see each other, perhaps he might be a better friend or teacher. And he says he could not understand how Emily can live so alone, without "even the companionship" of her dog.

Dickinson must have been pleased that Higginson thought her poems had "power" and that her thoughts had "quality," but think how disappointed she must have been that he still did not fully understand her or her poetry. Even after all this time, he thought that if he saw her often and was more involved in her personal life, he would better understand her. Dickinson must also have been disappointed that he felt she needed companionship more than understanding and appreciation as an artist.

EXERCISE ①

Read this passage from the selection. Use what you have learned in this lesson to answer the questions that follow it.

> People found her poetry puzzling. Editors and critics like Samuel Bowles, Dr. Holland, and Thomas Higginson thought most of it unsuitable to print. Emily was becoming resigned to this.
>
> Far from being discouraged, she was writing one poem after another. In 1862 alone, she wrote 365, among them the one beginning:
>
> *This is my letter to the World*
> *That never wrote to Me—*
>
> If her poems were published at all, she would remain anonymous. There would be no froglike croaking of her own name.
>
> *I'm nobody! Who are you?*
> *Are you—Nobody—too?*
> *Then there's a pair of us?*
> *Don't tell! They'd advertise—you know!*
>
> *How dreary—to be—Somebody!*
> *How public—like a Frog—*
> *To tell one's name—the livelong June—*
> *To an admiring Bog!*

1. Are the poems included in this passage examples of primary or secondary sources? Explain your answer.

2. Why do you think the author chose to include the poem, "I'm Nobody! Who are You?"

Now check your answers with your teacher. Review this lesson if you don't understand why an answer was incorrect.

WRITING ON YOUR OWN ①

In this exercise you will use what you learned in this lesson to select facts and information about your subject. Follow these steps

- Reread the notes you wrote for Writing: Developing a Biographical Sketch. Think about what primary or secondary sources you will use to give your reader information about your subject.
- Write one or two paragraphs describing an event that involved your subject. For example, imagine that your subject is a favorite uncle. In your notes you say that your uncle is special to you because he's always there to help everyone in your family and is always interested in everyone's opinion. Imagine that you want to tell how he helped your brother with his math homework. Your description of the event might read like this: "Eddie was desperate! His math homework was due tomorrow, and he was totally clueless about how to do the problems. In a panic he called my uncle. 'Help!' he screamed over the line. He could hear our uncle's kids shouting and laughing in the background. He heard dishes clattering. Eddie knew my uncle was busy—probably getting ready for dinner. But he explained his problem. In half an hour my uncle was at the door, ready to help."

- Imagine now that you were present when your uncle arrived and that you heard him say to Eddie, "I'm never too busy for you guys. If your grandfather hadn't helped me when I was a kid, I never would have passed math. Don't ever be afraid to ask questions." Using the exact words of your uncle in your biographical sketch would be relying on a primary source.

LESSON 2   INTERPRETATION AND THEME

Imagine that you kept a diary in which you wrote down everything that you did or that happened to you every day but not what your feelings and thoughts were about those events or experiences. If your diary were found later, people reading it might conclude that shopping at the mall meant as much to you as winning first prize at the school Science Fair. Unless you had interpreted, or explained, the meanings of those and other events and experiences included in your diary, people reading it would not understand their relative importance to you.

People who read biographies and autobiographies want to understand the lives of the people they read about. Therefore, a good biographer does much more than list the facts of a person's life. The biographer interprets—gives meaning to—those facts for the reader.

So how does a biographer, such as Barth, interpret facts? The first step is to establish a theme. As you learned in Unit 2, a theme is the underlying message or central idea of a piece of writing that the author wants you to understand. The theme of "The Soul Selects Her Own Society" might be stated like this: "Emily Dickinson expressed her deepest thoughts through her poetry. She hoped for, but never found, a companion who understood and shared her thoughts and deep feelings about life." By interpreting the facts she presents, explaining their meaning and evaluating their importance, Barth develops the theme of Dickinson's life story.

In this passage from the selection, the author gives you examples showing that people did not understand Emily or her poems.

There were no letters that day, but in the Original Poetry column in the *Springfield Republican* was her poem "Safe in their Alabaster Chambers." In bitter disappointment she stared at the lines she had written and rewritten so many times. The editors had changed some of the words. It was no longer her poem. She was glad she had not signed her name. . . .

Emily felt abandoned. More desperately than ever she turned to her poetry. At times she knew with deep certainty that it was good. With this came the feeling that life was good too.

At other times doubt crept in. Who said that her work was good? She herself, a few friends, a few editors. Editors distorted her verses for the sake of mere rhyme. Friends sometimes hinted that her poems, while remarkable, were strange "airy" things, not rooted enough in earth.

Perhaps she was no poet at all. Dark overwhelming forces seemed to rush toward her at the thought.

Look carefully at the facts in this passage and notice how Barth interprets them. Dickinson had gained enough confidence to submit one of her poems for publication in her friend Samuel Bowles's newspaper. She had carefully chosen each word in the poem. Someone at the newspaper had decided that they could "improve" her poem to make it better! Barth knows from her research that Dickinson was disappointed. To emphasize Dickinson's disappointment, Barth tells the reader that the poet was glad she had not signed her name.

Barth also reinforces her theme by telling you that Dickinson felt abandoned. There was only one way she felt free to express her feelings, and that was to "desperately turn to her poetry." It is not surprising that Dickinson felt disappointed, abandoned, and filled with self-doubt—editors had rewritten her poems, and friends had hinted that they didn't really understand them.

EXERCISE (2)

Read this passage from the selection. Use what you have learned in this lesson to answer the questions that follow it.

Emily read Mr. Higginson's reply with a mixture of excitement and disappointment. Though he praised the originality of her poems, it was clear that he didn't know what to make of them.

One of the poems was "We play at Paste—till qualified for Pearl." By including it, Emily hinted that she was no longer a beginner, but a poet, eager to perfect her art. Mr. Higginson, it was clear, thought otherwise. He urged her to master grammar, improve her rhyme, and try for smoother, more flowing lines.

Emily read the letter again. At least Mr. Higginson took her seriously. And she warmed to the kindness and sympathy between the lines.

1. Author Barth suggests that although Higginson praised the originality of Dickinson's poems, he made it clear that he didn't think Dickinson was a poet yet. What facts in the passage support this interpretation?

2. How does Higginson's reply to Emily relate to the theme of the selection?

Now check your answers with your teacher. Review this lesson if you don't understand why an answer was incorrect.

WRITING ON YOUR OWN ②

In this exercise you will use what you learned in this lesson to develop your theme. Follow these steps:

- Reread the paragraphs you wrote for Writing on Your Own 1. Do you see a theme—an underlying message, or central idea—in your description? Reread the sample sentences about "uncle and brother" in Writing on Your Own 1. Do you see a theme in all of the facts about your uncle? You might word that theme like this: "In spite of all the demands on his time, my uncle is a giving and caring person." All the facts about your uncle support that theme.
- Rewrite the first paragraph about your subject to include a sentence or two that expresses the theme that you want to convey to your readers. Then write three or four sentences that support that theme.
- Reread the sentences that you have written so far. Do both the events you've chosen to describe and the facts that you've included in the paragraph(s) reinforce your theme? Could you add any information that would help your reader better understand your theme?

LESSON ③ BIOGRAPHER'S OPINION

As a biographer researches and collects facts, he or she naturally forms an opinion about the subject. An *opinion* is what someone believes but cannot prove or disprove. The words Barth chooses, the facts she presents, and the way she organizes these facts all offer clues to her opinion of Dickinson. Her opinion is the basis for her interpretation of the events in the poet's life.

A writer's choice of words always provides clues to how the author feels about the people and events being described. Look, for example, at the first two paragraphs of the selection. Barth could have said, "Emily could bake delicious breads, and she sewed very well. For enjoyment, she would go to her garden." Now look at the way Barth describes those scenes. Emily's breads "brought a gleam of pleasure to her father's eye." In fact, he refused to eat bread baked by anyone else. He enjoyed having his daughter "cater" to him. And she didn't just enjoy her garden; Barth describes Dickinson's flower garden as "one of her greatest pleasures." Think of the vivid images you now have of Dickinson. The author created them by choosing words that bring images to mind.

Barth has also carefully selected which information she wants us to have. She doesn't tell about the room or the desk where Dickinson wrote her poetry. Instead, Barth gives information that will help readers see Dickinson as a real, living person. Can you see Dickinson making bread or surrounded by roses and lilies in the garden?

You can also see how Barth's opinion appears in what she writes, if you ask yourself what you think of Dickinson's sister, Vinnie. Where did your impression of Lavinia Dickinson come from?

Read the following passage, looking carefully at *what* and *how* the writer tells you about Lavinia. What can you infer about Barth's opinion of Dickinson's sister?

> Vinnie indulged Emily in her ways, willingly answering the doorbell, or delivering notes and flowers for her. With a flash of her dark eyes she quickly disposed of prying questions. "Why didn't Emily go to the sewing circle like everybody else?" "Why should she?" was Vinnie's retort. "If she's more contented to stay at home?"

Think about the words Barth used in this passage. Vinnie *indulged* her sister and *willingly* did things for her. These words imply that Vinnie loved her sister and wanted to please her. The passage even suggests that she supported Dickinson's desire for solitude. If Barth had written that Vinnie *allowed* Emily her ways and *grudgingly* did things for her, you would get a very different picture of Vinnie. Vinnie's dark eyes *flash* and she *retorts* to questions about Emily's behavior. Through the author's choice of words, you can actually see Vinnie defending her sister. It is clear that in Barth's opinion, Vinnie was not only devoted to and protective of her sister, but was also confident enough to say what she thought.

EXERCISE ③

Read this passage from the selection. Use what you have learned in this lesson to answer the questions that follow it.

Sometime in 1860, the year she was thirty years old, Emily fell in love, though who the man was no one has ever been sure. Some of the people who have studied her poems and letters think it was Charles Wadsworth, and others, Samuel Bowles. A man she called "Master" had begun appearing in letters and poems.

By now she had copied 150 poems into the little booklets. She had written about friendship, about life and death, about coming to know one's self. Now the poems were centering on love.

"'Tis so much joy! 'Tis so much joy!" one of the poems begins, and another, "Come slowly, Eden!" There were also poems in which she saw herself dressed in white or used the word *wife*, as if she considered herself married in spirit.

Then, within the year, Emily found out that the man she loved did not love her.

From almost delirious joy she plunged into deepest despair. For months afterward, in handwriting as chaotic as her state of mind, she poured her emotions into her writing. Poems such as "I felt a Funeral, in my Brain" show how overwhelmed she felt, and in some of her letters there are hints that she even feared losing her mind. No poem or letter was dated, but handwriting experts have guessed at the dates by a study of the changing script.

More and more of her words began with capital letters, and more were underlined. She used dashes more freely than ever, giving a breathless effect.

1. What specific words did Barth choose in describing Dickinson's feelings of happiness and then despair?

2. Barth chose to include references to two of Dickinson's poems in the foregoing passage to support her opinion of Dickinson's state of mind at the time she wrote them. How does each poem reflect what Dickinson was feeling at the time she wrote it?

Now check your answers with your teacher. Review this lesson if you don't understand why an answer was incorrect.

WRITING ON YOUR OWN ③

In this exercise you will use what you learned in this lesson to rewrite your paragraph(s), adding descriptive language and support for your opinion about your subject. Follow these steps:

• Reread the paragraph(s) you wrote in Writing on Your Own 1 and 2. Look again at the description of the event you have chosen. Does the description support your theme? Does it give the reader a clear image of your subject? What impression of your subject will it help your reader form?
• Now look at the words you used to describe the event and the person. Could you use more descriptive words that would create stronger images? Think about the words that Barth uses when she describes Vinnie or Dickinson's bread or garden.
• Rewrite your paragraph(s) to include more descriptive words.

DISCUSSION GUIDES

1. Skim the selection, looking for information and opinions about Sue Dickinson, the poet's sister-in-law. In a small group, discuss how you would describe Sue's character? What do you think Emily Dickinson thought of Sue? How would you describe the relationship between the two women? Share your group's opinion with the rest of the class.

2. As part of a small group, reread the poem that begins "I'm Nobody! Who are You?" on page 108. Imagine that you are a friend of Dickinson and that she has sent you this poem and asked for your reaction. As a group discuss what you would say to Dickinson in your reply. Put the group's collective thoughts into a single letter to the poet. Share the group's letter with your classmates.

3. Organize a class debate around the following questions: Do you think that a person is born with a certain character or personality already in place? Or do you think that people are shaped by their environment and the experiences they have? Discuss how changes in Dickinson's life might have affected her as a person or a poet. What would have happened if she had been born in a large city such as Boston or if her family had been poor?

WRITE A BIOGRAPHICAL SKETCH

In this unit you have learned how biographers gather facts about their subjects from both primary and secondary sources, interpret those facts to develop a theme, and express their own opinions through the facts they choose to include. Now you will write a biographical sketch about the subject you have chosen.

Follow these steps to complete your biographical sketch. If you have questions about the writing process, refer to Using the Writing Process (page 220).

- Gather and review the following pieces of writing you did for this unit: 1) the name of and notes about the person you chose to write about, 2) paragraph(s) using primary and secondary sources of information, 3) the revised paragraph(s) that includes several sentences stating and supporting your theme, 4) your rewritten paragraph(s) that contain descriptive language and supporting details.
- What you have written so far is sometimes called a firsthand biography. In a firsthand biography, you reveal your subject through your eyes and your response to that person. You have used a description of an incident or event, spoken words, and physical details to bring that person to life for your readers.
- Expand the biographical sketch you have already started. Think of other events in the subject's life or other experiences you have had with the subject. Use these to interpret your subject's life and to reinforce your theme.
- Remember to reveal your subject's character and personality through the events you describe. Be sure that every detail adds to your theme and supports your interpretation of your subject. Carefully choose the events and descriptive words that will help readers see your opinion of your subject.

- To help you think of additional events involving your subject, make a graphic organizer like the sample below on a sheet of paper. Write the name of your subject in the middle circle and events in the surrounding circles. Be sure that the events you add and the details you use to describe them support your theme. Add circles as needed.

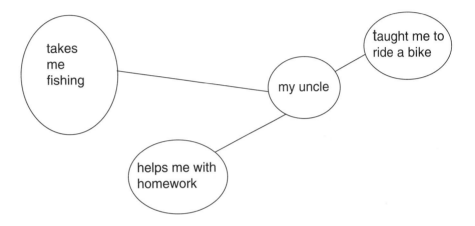

- When you have finished your biographical sketch, read it to classmates in a small group. Ask for their comments and any suggestions they might have to improve it. If you agree with any suggested changes, revise your sketch accordingly.
- Proofread your final draft for errors in spelling, grammar, punctuation, and capitalization. Make a final copy and save it in your writing portfolio.

Use of Language

Friendship

Excerpt from *I Know Why the Caged Bird Sings* by Maya Angelou

INTRODUCTION

BUILDING
BACKGROUND

In this unit you will read a selection from Maya Angelou's autobiography, *I Know Why the Caged Bird Sings*. Angelou is a well-known poet, author, playwright, actress, dancer, civil rights activist, producer, and director.

You learned in Unit 4 that an autobiography is the story of a real person's life written by that person. In her autobiography Angelou tells about her experiences growing up in a small, rural Southern town in the 1930s. At that time the nation was suffering from the Great Depression (1929–1939), and life was hard. Millions of people were out of work, and many others were barely earning enough to keep alive. Life was especially hard for African Americans. They had other hardships, besides the Great Depression, to deal with. In many places African Americans could only live in certain neighborhoods. It was against the law for them to use the same restaurants, public parks, schools, and public rest rooms as white people.

As you will see, despite the poverty and prejudice Angelou and her family faced, she grew to be strong and independent—and learned the value of love and friendship.

Who laughs at your jokes, listens to your ideas, and helps you solve your problems? Who lets you be yourself and likes you for who you are? A friend, that's who.

131

ABOUT THE AUTHOR

Maya Angelou was born on April 4, 1928, as Marguerite Johnson. She first came to be called "Maya" by members of her family. Her older brother, Bailey, began calling her "My Sister" soon after she was born. With time, this shortened to "My," and then eventually became "Maya."

When Angelou was three and Bailey four, their parents divorced, and the two children were sent to live with their father's mother, Mrs. Annie Johnson, in the small town of Stamps, Arkansas. Except for a few short periods, Angelou and her brother lived with "Momma" Johnson while they were growing up.

I Know Why the Caged Bird Sings was first published in 1969. The enormous popularity of her book brought Angelou widespread attention. People were fascinated and moved by her descriptions of growing up poor and black in a racially divided rural Southern town. Most of the book is filled with the young girl's detailed and colorful descriptions of daily life in and around her grandmother's general store in Stamps. Angelou was extraordinarily close to her brother, and both children were enveloped in the love of their strong, independent, and determined grandmother.

In several later volumes of her autobiography, the author continues the exciting story of her life and several careers. Angelou's work is admired by people all over the world. She has received many awards and honorary degrees and is considered an important spokesperson for the African-American community. President Bill Clinton honored Angelou by inviting her to be the main speaker at his inauguration ceremony in January 1993.

ABOUT THE LESSONS

The lessons that follow "Friendship" focus on the author's use of language. Despite the hardships in her life, Angelou learned to use language remarkably well. In "Friendship" she uses her skill as a writer not only to describe two experiences in her life but also to reveal her feelings about those experiences.

In this unit you will learn how Angelou uses imagery and figurative language to create vivid pictures of the people, places, and events she writes about. You'll also learn how she reveals much about herself through her choice of language.

WRITING: DEVELOPING AN AUTOBIOGRAPHICAL SKETCH

At the end of this unit, you will write an autobiographical sketch. The following suggestions will help you get started:

- Think of several memorable events or experiences from your past about which you have clear, detailed memories.
- List two or three of these experiences that you think others might be interested in reading about. Choose events or experiences that demonstrate, or explain, some important part of your character or personality. Beside each event or experience, write a sentence or two explaining *why* it was memorable.
- The event or experience you will write about later should give readers a clear picture of the people and events in the incident. It should also reveal something about you.

AS YOU READ   Think about these questions as you read the selection. They will help you understand and appreciate Angelou's use of language in "Friendship."

- How do the words and phrases Angelou uses in her descriptions help you to share in her experiences?
- What parts of this selection create the clearest images in your mind?
- What does Angelou think of two major characters in this selection—Louise and Tommy? What clues in her language help you know how she feels about each of them?

Friendship

Excerpt from *I Know Why the Caged Bird Sings* by Maya Angelou

"Acka Backa, Sody Cracka
Acka Backa, Boo
Acka Backa, Sody Cracka
I'm in love with you."

The sounds of tag beat through the trees while the top branches waved in contrapuntal[1] rhythms. I lay on a moment of green grass and telescoped the children's game to my vision. The girls ran about wild, now here, now there, never here, never was, they seemed to have no more direction than a splattered egg. But it was a shared if seldom voiced knowledge that all movements fitted, and worked according to a larger plan. I raised a platform for my mind's eye and marveled down on the outcome of "Acka Backa." The gay picnic dresses dashed, stopped and darted like beautiful dragonflies over a dark pool. The boys, black whips in the sunlight, popped behind the trees where their girls had fled, half hidden and throbbing in the shadows.

The summer picnic fish fry in the clearing by the pond was the biggest outdoor event of the year. Everyone was there.

---

[1] in music, a song or melody that plays above or below the main melody

All churches were represented, as well as the social groups (Elks, Eastern Star, Masons, Knights of Columbus, Daughters of Pythias), professional people (Negro teachers from Lafayette County) and all the excited children.

Musicians brought cigar-box guitars, harmonicas, juice harps, combs wrapped in tissue paper, and even bathtub basses.

The amount and variety of foods would have found approval on the menu of a Roman epicure.[2] Pans of fried chicken, covered with dishtowels, sat under benches next to a mountain of potato salad crammed with hard-boiled eggs. Whole rust-red sticks of bologna were clothed in cheesecloth. Homemade pickles and chow-chow, and baked country hams, aromatic with cloves and pineapples, vied for prominence. Our steady customers had ordered cold watermelons, so Bailey and I chugged the striped-green fruit into the Coca-Cola box and filled all the tubs with ice as well as the big black wash pot that Momma used to boil her laundry. Now they too lay sweating in the happy afternoon air.

The summer picnic gave ladies a chance to show off their baking hands. On the barbecue pit, chickens and spareribs sputtered in their own fat and a sauce whose recipe was guarded in the family like a scandalous affair. However, in the ecumenical[3] light of the summer picnic every true baking artist could reveal her prize to the delight and criticism of the town. Orange sponge cakes and dark brown mounds dripping Hershey's chocolate stood layer to layer with ice-white coconuts and light brown caramels. Pound cakes sagged with their buttery weight, and small children could no more resist licking the icings than their mothers could avoid slapping the sticky fingers.

Proven fishermen and weekend amateurs sat on the trunks of trees at the pond. They pulled the struggling bass and the silver perch from the swift water. A rotating crew of young

---

[2] a person with fine taste in food

[3] universal or worldwide, often applied to religion

girls scaled and cleaned the catch, and busy women in
starched aprons salted and rolled the fish in corn meal, then
dropped them in Dutch ovens trembling with boiling fat.

On one corner of the clearing a gospel group was rehears-
ing. Their harmony, packed as tight as sardines, floated over
the music of the county singers and melted into the songs of
the small children's ring games.

"Boys, don'chew let that ball fall on none of my cakes, you
do and it'll be me on you."

"Yes, m'am," and nothing changed. The boys continued
hitting the tennis ball with palings snatched from a fence and
running holes in the ground, colliding with everyone.

I had wanted to bring something to read, but Momma said
if I didn't want to play with the other children I could make
myself useful by cleaning fish or bringing water from the nearest well or wood for the barbecue.

I wandered into a retreat by accident. Signs with arrows
around the barbecue pit pointed MEN, WOMEN, CHILDREN
toward fading lanes, grown over since last year. Feeling ages
old and very wise at ten, I couldn't allow myself to be found
by small children squatting behind a tree. Neither did I have
the nerve to follow the arrow pointing the way for WOMEN. If
any grownup had caught me there, it was possible that she'd
think I was being "womanish" and would report me to
Momma, and I knew what I could expect from her. So when
the urge hit me to relieve myself, I headed toward another
direction. Once through the wall of sycamore trees I found
myself in a clearing ten times smaller than the picnic area,
and cool and quiet. After my business was taken care of, I
found a seat between two protruding roots of a black walnut
tree and leaned back on its trunk. Heaven would be like that
for the deserving. Maybe California too. Looking straight up
at the uneven circle of sky, I began to sense that I might be
falling into a blue cloud, far away. The children's voices and
the thick odor of food cooking over open fires were the hooks
I grabbed just in time to save myself.

Grass squeaked and I jumped at being found. Louise Kendricks walked into my grove. I didn't know that she too was escaping the gay spirit. We were the same age, and she and her mother lived in a neat little bungalow behind the school. Her cousins, who were in our age group, were wealthier and fairer, but I had secretly believed Louise to be the prettiest female in Stamps, next to Mrs. Flowers.

"What you doing sitting here by yourself, Marguerite?" She didn't accuse, she asked for information. I said that I was watching the sky. She asked, "What for?" There was obviously no answer to a question like that, so I didn't make up one. Louise reminded me of Jane Eyre.[4] Her mother lived in reduced circumstances, but she was genteel,[5] and though she worked as a maid I decided she should be called a governess and did so to Bailey and myself. (Who could teach a romantic dreamy ten-year-old to call a spade a spade?) Mrs. Kendricks could not have been very old, but to me all people over eighteen were adults and there could be no degree given or taken. They had to be catered to and pampered with politeness, then they had to stay in the same category of lookalike, soundalike and beingalike. Louise was a lonely girl, although she had plenty of playmates and was a ready partner for any ring game in the schoolyard.

Her face, which was long and dark chocolate brown, had a thin sheet of sadness over it, as light but as permanent as the viewing gauze on a coffin. And her eyes, which I thought her best feature, shifted quickly as if what they sought had just a second before eluded[6] her.

She had come near and the spotted light through the trees fell on her face and braids in running splotches. I had never noticed before, but she looked exactly like Bailey. Her hair was "good"—more straight than kinky—and her features had the regularity of objects placed by a careful hand.

---

[4] the heroine of an English novel by the same name

[5] polite or refined in manner

[6] escaped; slipped away from

She looked up—"Well, you can't see much sky from here." Then she sat down, an arm away from me. Finding two exposed roots, she laid thin wrists on them as if she had been in an easy chair. Slowly she leaned back against the tree. I closed my eyes and thought of the necessity of finding another place and the unlikelihood of there being another with all the qualifications that this one had. There was a little peal of a scream and before I could open my eyes Louise had grabbed my hand. "I was falling"—she shook her long braids—"I was falling in the sky."

I liked her for being able to fall in the sky and admit it. I suggested, "Let's try together. But we have to sit up straight on the count of five." Louise asked, "Want to hold hands? Just in case?" I did. If one of us did happen to fall, the other could pull her out.

After a few near tumbles into eternity (both of us knew what it was), we laughed at having played with death and destruction and escaped.

Louise said, "Let's look at that old sky while we're spinning." We took each other's hands in the center of the clearing and began turning around. Very slowly at first. We raised our chins and looked straight at the seductive patch of blue. Faster, just a little faster, then faster, faster yet. Yes, help, we were falling. Then eternity won, after all. We couldn't stop spinning or falling until I was jerked out of her grasp by greedy gravity and thrown to my fate below—no, above, not below. I found myself safe and dizzy at the foot of the sycamore tree. Louise had ended on her knees at the other side of the grove.

This was surely the time to laugh. We lost but we hadn't lost anything. First we were giggling and crawling drunkenly toward each other and then we were laughing out loud uproariously. We slapped each other on the back and shoulders and laughed some more. We had made a fool or a liar out of something, and didn't that just beat all?

In daring to challenge the unknown with me, she

became my first friend. We spent tedious[7] hours teaching ourselves the Tut language. You (Yak oh you) know (kack nug oh wug) what (wack hash a tut). Since all the other children spoke Pig Latin, we were superior because Tut was hard to speak and even harder to understand. At last I began to comprehend what girls giggled about. Louise would rattle off a few sentences to me in the unintelligible[8] Tut language and would laugh. Naturally I laughed too. Snickered, really, understanding nothing. I don't think she understood half of what she was saying herself, but, after all, girls have to giggle. . . .

In school one day, a girl whom I barely knew and had scarcely spoken to brought me a note. The intricate fold indicated that it was a love note. I was sure she had the wrong person, but she insisted. Picking the paper loose, I confessed to myself that I was frightened. Suppose it was somebody being funny? Suppose the paper would show a hideous beast and the word YOU written over it. Children did that sometimes just because they claimed I was stuck-up. Fortunately I had got permission to go to the toilet—an outside job—and in the reeking gloom I read:

Dear Friend, M. J.

Times are hard and friends are few
I take great pleasure in writing you
Will you be my Valentine?
Tommy Valdon

I pulled my mind apart. Who? Who was Tommy Valdon? Finally a face dragged itself from my memory. He was the nice-looking brown-skinned boy who lived across the pond.

---

[7] tiresome

[8] impossible to understand

As soon as I had pinned him down, I began to wonder, Why? Why me? Was it a joke? But if Tommy was the boy I remembered, he was a very sober person and a good student. Well, then, it wasn't a joke. All right, what evil dirty things did he have in mind? My questions fell over themselves, an army in retreat. Haste, dig for cover. Protect your flanks. Don't let the enemy close the gap between you. What did a Valentine do, anyway?

Starting to throw the paper in the foul-smelling hole, I thought of Louise. I could show it to her. I folded the paper back in the original creases and went back to class. There was no time during the lunch period since I had to run to the Store and wait on customers. The note was in my sock and every time Momma looked at me, I feared that her church gaze might have turned into X-ray vision and she could not only see the note and read its message but would interpret it as well. I felt myself slipping down a sheer cliff of guilt, and a second time I nearly destroyed the note but there was no opportunity. The take-up bell rang and Bailey raced me to school, so the note was forgotten. But serious business is serious, and it had to be attended to. After classes I waited for Louise. She was talking to a group of girls, laughing. But when I gave her our signal (two waves of the left hand) she said goodbye to them and joined me in the road. I didn't give her the chance to ask what was on my mind (her favorite question); I simply gave her the note. Recognizing the fold she stopped smiling. We were in deep waters. She opened the letter and read it aloud twice. "Well, what do you think?"

I said, "What do I think? That's what I'm asking you? What is there to think?"

"Looks like he wants you to be his valentine."

"Louise, I can read. But what does it mean?"

"Oh, you know. His valentine. His love."

There was that hateful word again. That treacherous word that yawned up at you like a volcano.

"Well, I won't. Most decidedly I won't. . . .

"Well, don't answer him then, and that's the end of it." I was a little relieved that she thought it could be gotten rid of so quickly. I tore the note in half and gave her a part. Walking down the hill we minced[9] the paper in a thousand shreds and gave it to the wind.

Two days later a monitor came into my classroom. She spoke quietly to Miss Williams, our teacher. Miss Williams said, "Class, I believe you remember that tomorrow is Valentine's Day, so named for St. Valentine, the martyr, who died around A.D. 270 in Rome. The day is observed by exchanging tokens of affection, and cards. The eighth-grade children have completed theirs and the monitor is acting as mailman. You will be given cardboard, ribbon, and red tissue paper during the last period today so that you may make your gifts. Glue and scissors are here at the work table. Now, stand when your name is called."

She had been shuffling the colored envelopes and calling names for some time before I noticed. I had been thinking of yesterday's plain invitation and the expeditious way Louise and I took care of it.

We who were being called to receive valentines were only slightly more embarrassed than those who sat and watched as Miss Williams opened each envelope. "Helen Gray." Helen Gray, a tall, dull girl from Louisville, flinched. "Dear Valentine"—Miss Williams began reading the badly rhymed childish drivel. I seethed with shame and anticipation and yet had time to be offended at the silly poetry that I could have bettered in my sleep.

"Margue-you-reete Ann Johnson. My goodness, this looks more like a letter than a valentine. 'Dear Friend, I wrote you a letter and saw you tear it up with your friend Miss L. I don't believe you meant to hurt my feelings so whether you answer or not you will always be my valentine. T.V.'"

---

[9] cut or chopped into very small pieces

"Class"—Miss Williams smirked and continued lazily without giving us permission to sit down—"although you are only in the seventh grade, I'm sure you wouldn't be so presumptuous[10] as to sign a letter with an initial. But here is a boy in the eighth grade, about to graduate—blah, blah, blooey, blah. You may collect your valentines and these letters on your way out."

It was a nice letter and Tommy had beautiful penmanship. I was sorry I tore up the first. His statement that whether I answered him or not would not influence his affection reassured me. . . . I told Louise that the next time he came to the Store I was going to say something extra nice to him. Unfortunately the situation was so wonderful to me that each time I saw Tommy I melted in delicious giggles and was unable to form a coherent[11] sentence. After a while he stopped including me in his general glances.

REVIEWING AND INTERPRETING

Record your answers to these questions in your personal literature notebook. Follow the directions for each part.

REVIEWING Try to complete each of these sentences without looking back at the selection.

Recalling Facts 1. Marguerite and Louise Kendricks became friends at
  a. school.
  b. the store.
  c. their church.
  d. the picnic.

Understanding Main Ideas 2. For Marguerite, the summer picnic fish fry was important because
  a. it was a chance to run wild.
  b. she made her first friend there.
  c. it gave her a chance to earn money.
  d. there was plenty to eat there.

Identifying Sequence 3. Marguerite received a note from Tommy Valdon
  a. before the picnic.
  b. before Valentine's Day.
  c. on Valentine's Day.
  d. after the teacher read his valentine aloud.

Finding Supporting Details 4. You can tell that Marguerite did not expect to be part of the picnic activities because
  a. she wanted to bring something to read.
  b. she didn't bake anything.
  c. she helped Bailey with the watermelons.
  d. Momma Johnson told her to make herself useful.

Getting Meaning from Context

5. "I had been thinking of yesterday's plain invitation and the expeditious way Louise and I took care of it." In this sentence, *expeditious* means
a. efficient.
b. cruel.
c. silly.
d. sneaky.

INTERPRETING To complete these items, you may look back at the selection if you'd like.

Making Inferences

6. From the way Marguerite describes her teacher, you can infer that Miss Williams was
a. not very pretty.
b. jealous of the girls' valentines.
c. very critical of others.
d. kindhearted.

Generalizing

7. From this selection you can tell that Marguerite
a. was very attractive.
b. had difficulty making friends her own age.
c. was mature for her age.
d. wished she had more friends.

Recognizing Fact and Opinion

8. Which of the following is a statement of fact?
a. "Heaven would be like that for the deserving."
b. "The summer picnic fish fry in the clearing by the pond was the biggest outdoor event of the year."
c. "The amount and variety of foods would have found approval on the menu of a Roman epicure."
d. "It was a nice letter and Tommy had beautiful penmanship."

Identifying Cause and Effect

9. Marguerite and Louise became friends because
  a. they both liked to read.
  b. they both had active, creative imaginations.
  c. they both were poor.
  d. Louise gave Maguerite good advice.

Drawing Conclusions

10. From this selection you can conclude that Maguerite
  a. showed her valentine to Bailey.
  b. respected her teacher's opinion.
  c. sent Tommy a valentine in return.
  d. trusted Louise's advice.

Now check your answers with your teacher. Study the items you answered incorrectly. What skills are they checking? Talk with your teacher about ways to work on these skills.

Use of Language

All good writers are aware of the power of language. Because Angelou is a poet, she chooses every word with special care, to create exactly the image or to arouse the feeling that she wants the reader to experience.

Writers use language in many ways to create interesting, colorful images and to affect readers' feelings. In the lessons that follow, we will talk about three of those ways:

1. **Imagery and Word Choice** Writers use language to appeal to the senses—sight, hearing, touch, smell, and taste. By doing so, writers create images in the mind and affect our feelings.

2. **Figurative Language** Writers use certain words and phrases in unusual ways to create strong, vivid images. Sometimes they give these words and phrases meanings that are different from their usual meanings.

3. **Tone** By paying attention to the ways a writer uses language, you can discover the writer's tone, or attitude, toward his or her subject.

LESSON 1 IMAGERY AND WORD CHOICE

Imagery is the use of words or phrases that appeal to one or more of the senses—sight, hearing, taste, smell, and touch. Most images in writing are visual. They appeal to the sense of sight to make the reader "see" something. But writers also use imagery to help readers experience the way things sound, taste, smell, and touch. Angelou has a poet's gift for creating images—pictures and other sensations in the reader's mind.

Painters choose the colors and texture of their paints to reproduce the details of what they see *and* to communicate their feelings about it. Writers work in the same way, using words instead of paints. The English language contains many words that have similar meanings. Some words are more specific than others—*oak* is a more specific word than *tree*. Good writers try to use the most specific words they can. What does each of the following expressions suggest to you: *girl, child, maiden, teenager, youth,* and *young woman*? All of them could be used to describe the same person, yet each one suggests something different and creates a different mental picture of this person.

Choosing just the right words enables the writer to recreate in the reader's mind what the writer saw or felt. Through her use of imagery, Angelou lets her audience experience the events she describes as she experienced them.

Read this paragraph from "Friendship," noticing how Angelou chooses words to create a vivid mental picture and to share a feeling.

> The summer picnic gave ladies a chance to show off their baking hands. On the barbecue pit, chickens and spareribs sputtered in their own fat and a sauce whose recipe was guarded in the family like a scandalous affair. However, in the ecumenical light of the summer picnic every true baking artist could reveal her prize to the delight and criticism of the town. Orange sponge cakes and dark brown mounds dripping Hershey's chocolate stood layer to layer with ice-white coconuts and light brown caramels. Pound cakes sagged with their buttery weight, and small children could no more resist licking the icings than their mothers could avoid slapping the sticky fingers.

As you were reading, could you picture all of this delicious food spread out before you? Could you almost smell the chicken and spareribs being barbecued? Maybe you could even hear them "sputtering in their own fat" over the barbecue pit. Perhaps you could even taste them. Imagine how differently you would picture the scene in your mind if Angelou had simply said, "Chicken and spareribs were being cooked."

Look at the specific details Angelou uses to help the reader "see" the picnic cakes. The sponge cakes are "orange." Instead of saying, "There were several chocolate cakes," she writes that "dark brown mounds dripping Hershey's chocolate stood layer by layer." Pound cakes "sagged"—not just with their weight, but with their "buttery weight." By the time we reach the end of the paragraph, we don't blame the children who can't resist sticking their fingers into the icings.

The children aren't the only ones impressed by this food. The people who prepared it are proud of their efforts. They have a chance to "show off their baking hands." Angelou says that "every true baking artist could reveal her prize to the delight and criticism of the town." Words and phrases like these tell readers much more effectively how these people feel than simply saying "The ladies were proud of the food they had prepared."

What can you infer about how the writer herself feels about this scene? It's not hard to tell. Look at the words she chooses. You can tell that she enjoys recalling and describing that experience.

EXERCISE ①

Read this passage from the selection. Use what you have learned in this lesson to answer the questions that follow it.

The amount and variety of foods would have found approval on the menu of a Roman epicure. Pans of fried chicken, covered with dishtowels, sat under benches next to a mountain of potato salad crammed with hard-boiled eggs. Whole rust-red sticks of bologna were clothed in cheesecloth. Homemade pickles and chow-chow, and baked country hams, aromatic with cloves and pineapples, vied for prominence. Our steady customers had ordered cold water-melons, so Bailey and I chugged the striped-green fruit into the Coca-Cola box and filled all the tubs with ice as well as the big black wash pot that Momma used to boil her laundry. Now they too lay sweating in the happy afternoon air.

1. What words or phrases in this passage appeal to the senses? Find at least one word or phrase that appeals to each of the five senses.

2. Copy the graphic organizer that follows on a sheet of paper. Think about a dinner you had recently that you really enjoyed. In the organizer try to list details about your dinner that appeal to each of the five senses.

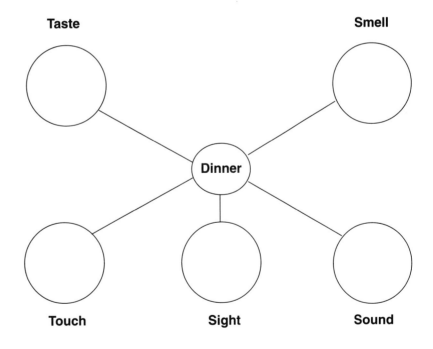

Now check your answers with your teacher. Review this lesson if you don't understand why an answer was incorrect.

WRITING ON YOUR OWN ①

In this exercise you will use what you have learned in this lesson to write two or three paragraphs describing a memorable event or experience in your life. Follow these steps:

- Review the ideas you listed for Writing: Developing an Autobiographical Sketch. Choose one event or experience that you would like to develop. Before you write, think about the important facts and details you need to include. What people will you describe? What settings? What things?

- Now write two or three paragraphs describing the event or experience you have chosen. Be sure to include *why* this event or experience was a memorable one in your life. For example, you might write about an overnight camping trip during which you overcame your fear of the dark. Or you might relate a humorous incident in which your determination always to tell the truth caused you or someone else to be embarrassed.

- When you have finished writing your paragraphs, reread them. Look at the way you have described each person, place, or thing that you mentioned. Could you use a more accurate or colorful word or words to describe them? For example, if you were writing about a camping trip, you might change *guide* to *veteran woodsman* and *tall trees* to *towering pines.* Can you add more descriptive words? For example, depending on the circumstances, you could write *brave trail companions* or *faint-hearted trail companions.* Finally, look at the words you have used to describe actions. Can you think of more colorful or accurate replacements? For example, you might change *I stayed awake* to *I was frozen in bug-eyed wakefulness.*

LESSON ②   FIGURATIVE LANGUAGE

When words or phrases are used figuratively, they have meanings other than their usual, or literal, meanings. If an author writes "The full moon gazed down upon us," he or she doesn't literally mean that the moon can actually see. The author is using figurative language to create an image, or picture in your mind. *Figurative language* refers to words and phrases used in unusual ways to create strong, vivid images. Figurative language focuses attention on certain ideas or compares unlike things. In this lesson you will see how Angelou uses four kinds of figurative language.

Simile   A *simile* is a direct comparison between two basically unlike things that have some quality in common. When you say things such as "Megan swims like a fish" or "My hands are like icicles," you are using similes. The comparison is made using the words *like*, *as*, *than*, or *resembles*, and sometimes the verbs *appear* or *seem*. Writers use similes to produce a vivid new way of looking at one of the things. You use similes all the time, probably without even realizing it.

In the first paragraph of this selection, Angelou uses two similes to describe the girls at the picnic. In the first she says that the running girls "seemed to have no more direction than a splattered egg." If you've ever dropped an egg and have seen how it splatters, you can immediately picture in your mind what she means: like the egg splattering about, the girls are flying off in all directions at once. The second simile is even more effective. Angelou describes the girls in their gay picnic dresses this way: they "dashed, stopped, and darted like beautiful dragonflies over a dark pool." Picture for a moment a dragonfly, with its bright rainbow-colored wings, darting first one way and then another through the air. By comparing the girls to dragonflies fluttering over a dark pool, Angelou is painting a picture in your mind of the girls flitting here and there, their brightly colored dresses standing out sharply against the dark background of the trees.

Metaphor   A *metaphor* is a comparison made between two basically unlike things without using a word of comparison such as *like* or *as*. A metaphor suggests that one thing is another. If you said "Sometimes my friend Ted is a mule," you wouldn't mean that Ted is actually an animal. You would mean that sometimes he displays the stubbornness for which mules are famous.

Look again at the first paragraph of the selection. After using two similes to describe the girls, Angelou creates a metaphor to describe the boys. She writes, "The boys, black whips in the sunlight, popped behind the trees where their girls had fled, half hidden and throbbing in the shadows." The boys are not really whips, but Angelou's image creates a clear picture in your mind of their thinness, their blackness, and their quick, snappy motions as they popped behind the trees.

Hyperbole   *Hyperbole* is a figure of speech in which the truth is deliberately exaggerated in order to express an idea or feeling. "I have a ton of homework to do" and "I've told you that a million times" are examples of hyperbole. In each sentence, the speaker is deliberately exaggerating, or overstating, the truth to make a point. When Angelou describes the boys running around hitting the tennis ball at the picnic, as "running holes in the ground." She knows that the reader won't think the boys are really making holes in the ground. By exaggerating the image so vividly, however, she hopes to create a clear and instant picture of the boys running so fast that their feet are kicking up dirt.

When Angelou says that she feared Momma's gaze might have "turned into X-ray vision," we have a very clear sense of how powerful she feels her grandmother is. Such language is much more effective than "I hoped Momma wouldn't guess that I had a note in my pocket." When the author says that she and Louise had "a few near tumbles into eternity," you know just how scary and exciting their imaginative game has become.

Personification Another kind of figurative language is personification. *Personification* is a figure of speech in which an animal, an object, or an idea is given the characteristics of a person. Sometimes writers use personification to add humor or to describe abstract ideas such as freedom, truth, and beauty.

The following sentences are examples of personification: "Lightning danced across the sky" and "Fear gripped my heart as the dangerous storm approached." In those sentences, both *lightning* and *fear* are given characteristics of a person. Lightning cannot really *dance*, nor can *fear* actually *grip* anything. Does the use of personification in those sentences create a vivid image of the approaching storm?

In the paragraph that describes how Marguerite and Louise twirled around in the sunshine, Angelou writes: "We couldn't stop spinning or falling until I was jerked out of her grasp by greedy gravity. . . ." Gravity, of course, can't grasp or be greedy. The idea that gravity *wants* to grab Marguerite back is very important at this point in the story. She left the picnic to be alone with her imagination. When Louise arrives, both lonely girls take an imaginative flight together. But people can't always live in their imaginations. When gravity (reality) jerks Marguerite back, she finds herself literally and figuratively back on the ground again, and she finds herself with a friend in the real world.

EXERCISE ②

Use what you have learned in this lesson to answer these questions.

1. What kind of figurative language does Angelou use in this sentence: "On the barbecue pit, chickens and spareribs sputtered in their own fat and a sauce whose recipe was guarded in the family like a scandalous affair."

2. In that sentence what two basically unlike things does Angelou compare? In what way does she mean the two things are alike?

Now check your answers with your teacher. Review this lesson if you don't understand why an answer was incorrect.

WRITING ON YOUR OWN ②

In this exercise you will use what you learned in this lesson to add figurative language to your description of a memorable event or experience in your life. Follow these steps:

- Reread the paragraphs you wrote for Writing on Your Own 1. Think about what you have learned in this lesson about the uses of figurative language. Now close your eyes and think about the setting and each person and thing you have described.
- Try to make an unusual comparison, using a simile or a metaphor that will help your reader experience what you saw, heard, touched, tasted, or smelled.
- Pick something that you can exaggerate for emphasis. For example, you might say, "After an entire day on the trail, my tortured toes were 10 throbbing, red-hot coals."
- Now consider using personification in your description. If there is a thing or an abstract idea in your description that seems too vague or general, try to give it some human characteristics. For example, you might say, "My tent fought back my every effort to keep it upright in the wind" or "Fatigue told me loudly and clearly that it was time to rest."
- When you have finished rewriting your paragraphs, reread them. Try to imagine that you are the reader for a moment. Might anything you wrote puzzle or confuse someone unfamiliar with what you are describing?

LESSON ③ TONE

Tone is a writer's attitude toward his or her subject or audience. You can sense a writer's tone by looking at the language he or she uses in describing people, places, and events. Sometimes the writer's tone can also reveal something about him- or herself. In "Friendship" Angelou describes people and places from her childhood, but in doing this she also reveals her attitude toward herself.

Look at how Angelou describes her meeting with Louise in the grove during the picnic. Reread the eight paragraphs on pages 137–138 that begin with "What you doing here sitting by yourself, Marguerite?" and end with "We had made a fool or a liar out of something, and didn't that just beat all?" What is Marguerite's attitude toward Louise when she first arrives and how does it change? What does this tell us about Marguerite herself?

When Louise first walks into the grove, Marguerite is irritated that someone else has found her spot. Although she thinks that Louise is pretty and a nice person, Marguerite immediately thinks about "the necessity of finding another place and the unlikelihood of there being another with all the qualifications that this one had." The author describes Louise as lonely and sad, but the reader can tell from Marguerite's reactions that she herself is also pretty much of a loner.

What happens next is important. Louise stares up into the sky. She gives a little scream and says that she is falling into the sky. This is the same sensation that Marguerite had felt a moment before. Angelou writes, "I liked her for being able to fall in the sky and admit it." This marks an important change in Marguerite's attitude toward Louise. Marguerite suggests, "Let's try together," and Louise replies, "Want to hold hands? Just in case?" Each lonely girl begins to trust the other a bit. The author's tone (shown in the character's attitude toward Louise) changes, because Marguerite discovers that she and Louise share the same kind of strong imagination.

EXERCISE (3)

Read this passage from the selection. Use what you have learned in this lesson to answer the questions that follow.

> "Class"—Miss Williams smirked and continued lazily without giving us permission to sit down— "although you are only in the seventh grade, I'm sure you wouldn't be so presumptuous as to sign a letter with an initial. But here is a boy in the eighth grade, about to graduate—blah, blah, blooey, blah. You may collect your valentines and these letters on your way out."
>
> It was a nice letter and Tommy had beautiful penmanship. I was sorry I tore up the first. His statement that whether I answered him or not would not influence his affection reassured me. . . . I told Louise that the next time he came to the Store I was going to say something extra nice to him. Unfortunately the situation was so wonderful to me that each time I saw Tommy I melted in delicious giggles and was unable to form a coherent sentence. After a while he stopped including me in his general glances.

1. Describe Marguerite's attitude toward Miss Williams in this passage. What words and phrases suggest the author's tone?

2. How would you describe Marguerite's attitude toward Tommy in the last paragraph? What emotions do you think she was feeling?

Now check your answers with your teacher. Review this lesson if you don't understand why an answer was incorrect.

WRITING ON YOUR OWN ③

In this exercise you will use what you learned in this lesson about tone to rewrite and expand your descriptive paragraphs. Follow these steps:

- Reread the description you wrote for Writing on Your Own 2. Think about what you learned about tone in this lesson. Write one or two sentences that summarize your attitude toward this experience or event as it was happening. Then write one or two more sentences that summarize your present attitude toward that same experience now that you are older. For example, if you were writing about the camping trip during which you overcame your fear of the dark, you might write, "At the time I was sure my life would end when I opened the tent flap. Now I realize that the chances of being attacked by vengeful pirates or hungry vampires were pretty slim."
- Look carefully at the paragraphs you have written. Can you revise or add to your description to give the reader clues to your attitude toward what was happening to you at the time? Can you change or add language that tells how you *felt*? Look at words that describe what you did. Can you add modifiers that show *how* you acted? For example, did you do something *cautiously, bravely, secretively, with your heart in your mouth*, or *as though your fingers were all thumbs*?

DISCUSSION GUIDES

1. The selection that you read is one chapter from *I Know Why the Caged Bird Sings.* In a small group discuss why Angelou decided to write about these two incidents in the same chapter. Is there a theme that connects the two sets of events? What does she have to say about this theme? Share your observations with the rest of the class.

2. When Angelou describes Louise's mother, she says, "To me all people over eighteen were adults and there could be no degree given or taken. They all had to be catered to and pampered with politeness, then they had to stay in the same category of lookalike, soundalike, and beingalike." As a class discuss what Marguerite means by this? Do you agree with her? Why or why not?

3. With a partner discuss how the other two people involved in this selection might have pictured Marguerite. What do you think Louise thought about her? How would she have described her to someone else. What do you think attracted Tommy to Marguerite. How would he have described her? Discuss the similarities and differences between Tommy's and Louise's views and your own view of Marguerite. Share your descriptions with the class.

WRITE AN AUTOBIOGRAPHICAL SKETCH

In this unit you have seen how Angelou uses language to create vivid images of people, places, things, and events. Now you will use what you have learned, in order to write an autobiographical sketch.

Follow these steps to complete your sketch. If you have any questions about the writing process, refer to Using the Writing Process (page 220).

- Review the following pieces of writing you did in this unit: 1) the list of memorable events or experiences and the reasons you chose them, 2) the paragraphs describing the event or experience, 3) the rewritten paragraphs using figurative language, 4) the revised paragraphs incorporating your tone, or attitude.
- Now write a one- or two-paragraph introduction for your autobiographical sketch. Use your introduction to describe yourself. Writing an autobiography is about taking a clear look at yourself, so try to be specific in describing what you are like.
- Next write a brief paragraph that connects your introduction to the descriptive paragraphs you have already written. Try to show how what you have said about yourself in the introduction relates to the event or experience you are describing in detail.
- Add a short concluding paragraph, briefly summarizing for your readers what this event or experience means to you.
- Read your completed autobiographical sketch to a classmate, friend, or family member. Ask your "audience" to comment on your sketch and to suggest ways that you might improve it. If any suggested changes seem warranted, revise your sketch accordingly.
- Proofread your final draft for errors in spelling, grammar, punctuation, and capitalization. Make a final copy and save it in your writing portfolio.

The Persuasive Essay

Sin Papeles

○

Introduction to
The Uncertain Journey: Stories of Illegal Aliens in El Norte by Margaret Poynter

INTRODUCTION

BUILDING
BACKGROUND

"Give me your tired, your poor,
Your huddled masses yearning to breathe free,
The wretched refuse of your teeming shore.
Send these, the homeless, tempest-tossed to me.
I lift my lamp beside the golden door."

These words are from the poem "The New Colossus" by Emma Lazarus. The complete poem, printed on a plaque at the base of the Statue of Liberty—like the statue itself—once symbolized America's mission to be a home for immigrants.

Until the early 1900s the United States welcomed all immigrants. As a young and growing country, it needed people to build railroads, work in factories, and farm the land. Millions of people came from countries such as China, Great Britain, Germany, Ireland, Italy, the Scandinavian countries, Czechoslovakia, Poland, Hungary, and Russia. By 1917, however, most Americans were convinced that there were too many immigrants. People seemed to forget that they themselves had once been, or were descendants of, immigrants to the United States. They wanted to stop the flow of "outsiders." This attitude resulted in the passage of the Immigration Act of

Every year, thousands of people from Mexico and Central America cross the border between the United States and Mexico illegally. Only about 30 miles of the 2,000-mile border between the two countries is fenced.

1924, which limited the number of people, and the number from each specific country, who could enter the United States. For example, more people could enter the United States from Great Britain or Germany than could from eastern Europe or South America. In 1968 the immigration laws were finally changed in favor of a first-come–first-served policy.

"Sin Papeles," the essay you will read, is about illegal aliens—people who entered the United States without following approved procedures. These *sin papeles*, "those without papers," are mostly from Central and South America. The countries they come from are poor, and there are very few jobs available for them there. They come to *El Norte*—the North—looking for jobs and a better life. Some people believe that these illegal aliens are damaging the economy of the United States. Others fear that the great numbers of immigrants from the south will change American culture and traditions and that English will no longer be the primary language. Still others believe that our immigration policies need to change so that more people can legally enter the country.

The concerns over illegal aliens have become a major social issue. You will find that most people have a very strong opinion either in favor of or against the *sin papeles*. The essay will help you better understand the problem and perhaps help you form your own opinion about this issue.

ABOUT THE AUTHOR

Margaret Poynter was born into a family of writers. Her father and her grandmother were writers, so she was constantly exposed to books and the "pecking of typewriters." In school she liked writing essays, and she looked forward to book reports because they involved both reading and writing.

Poynter's career as a writer did not seriously start until she left her full-time job as a waitress and the last of her four children was in high school. Her advice to those who want to become writers is "Don't give up. A writer must keep on writing in spite of rejection slips and other setbacks and obstacles. I wrote my first book between the kitchen table and the broom closet because my sons' rock music group had taken over the rest of the house. . . . I find time to write, despite the hours I still spend working in a restaurant and at our local paper."

Poynter has written more than 15 books and has contributed more than 60 stories and articles to magazines.

ABOUT THE LESSONS

The lessons that follow "Sin Papeles" focus on how to evaluate opinions in a persuasive essay. When reading a persuasive essay, readers may or may not agree with the author's position or opinions on an issue. But before we make our judgments, we need to identify the author's opinions and decide whether they are supported by facts.

In "Sin Papeles" the author wants to provide information *and* persuade readers to agree with her opinion. One way an author persuades is by presenting strong, logical reasons for his or her opinion. Another way is to appeal to the emotions.

WRITING: DEVELOPING A PERSUASIVE ESSAY

In this unit you will learn how to develop a persuasive argument—how to convince readers that your opinions are correct. At the end of the unit, you will use this argument to write a persuasive essay. The following suggestions will help you get started:

• Think about topics or issues that you have strong feelings about. Perhaps you feel strongly that people should try to do more to help save the environment. Do you believe that everyone should recycle trash? Do you believe that no one should smoke in public places? Should public-school students be required to wear uniforms? Maybe you feel strongly that people should do more to stop the "greenhouse effect." On what topic or issue would you like to convince other people to take action?

- List two or three issues that you feel strongly about. Now think about why you would want to convince others to take your stand about these issues. Jot down notes after each issue on your list.

AS YOU READ   Think about these questions as you read the essay. They will help you identify the author's opinions about illegal aliens in the United States and decide how well she supports them.

- What is the main opinion Poynter expresses in her essay?
- What kinds of information does the author give to support this opinion? Does she support her opinion effectively?
- Does the author convince, or persuade, you to think about her subject in a different way?
- Does the author's use of language affect the way you think about the subject? What words or phrases does the author use to affect the way you feel?

Sin Papeles

⊙

Introduction to
The Uncertain Journey: Stories of Illegal Aliens in El Norte by Margaret Poynter

They clear the tables, wash the dishes, and mop the floors of our restaurants. They wash our cars, manufacture our clothing, do our laundry, dig our ditches, and man our factory assembly lines. They plant and harvest our crops, mow our lawns, and toil in our canneries and fish-packing plants. They stand on our street corners selling fruit or offering to shine our shoes.

To get these menial,[1] tedious, low-paying, often physically grueling[2] jobs, these men and women walk, crawl, and swim across our southern border, facing hardships and dangers in the darkness of night. They come from such impoverished[3] countries as Mexico, Guatemala, Colombia, and Haiti, where at least half of them live in dirt-floored hovels with no plumbing or electricity. Only a few understand English; most of them can't read or write their native language. The jobs they find here are dreams come true. The money they earn may make the difference between whether their children remain uneducated or go to school. It may even determine whether those children will live or will die from lack of food and medical care.

---

[1] suited to a servant; lowly

[2] tiring to the point of exhaustion

[3] made very poor

They are the tens of thousands of *sin papeles*, "those without papers," who enter the United States illegally every year.

Before the start of the twentieth century, there was no such thing as an illegal alien in the United States. All immigrants were welcomed because our young, growing country needed people to work in our factories and to farm our vast expanse of empty land. Then, as our cities grew crowded, and our good farmland scarce, laws were passed to control the number of people who were allowed to become legal residents and, thus, to take jobs. To enforce those laws, the United States Immigration and Naturalization Service (INS) was created. The United States Border Patrol is the "police force" of the INS. Its officers have the job of apprehending illegal aliens as they attempt to enter our country.

Most of the people who enter the United States illegally are Mexicans. For them, getting into *El Norte* is just a matter of walking or swimming across a largely unprotected border. Salvadorans, Colombians, and Jamaicans, however, usually hire a *coyote*, a smuggler of people, to provide transportation and guidance. In the plazas, bus depots, and coffee shops of their countries, the *pollos*, "chickens" or "those who run," make contact with *coyotes*. Money changes hands, and a time and place of departure is arranged.

Most *coyotes* are honest, with a handshake guaranteeing the eventual success of their mission. However, the possibility of dealing with a dishonest *coyote* is the first hazard many illegal aliens must face. Some *pollos* have been stranded in life-threatening situations, and smugglers sometimes extort more money from their former clients by threatening to report them to *la migra*, someone who works for the immigration service.

Because of the numbers of men and women who look to *El Norte* as the answer to their pressing problems, *coyotes* do a brisk business. Some of them work individually, recruiting a few people at a time. Others belong to a far-flung network of smugglers who contract with the owners of large ranches and farms to furnish crews of workers.

The *coyote* networks are remarkably efficient. Several years ago, the border patrol started using helicopters in the area between Tijuana, Mexico, and San Ysidro, California. Within a week, *coyotes* in Quito, Ecuador, were telling their clients how to avoid being spotted by the aircrafts' searchlights.

There's a border patrol checkpoint twenty miles to the north of San Diego, California, but there isn't enough money or manpower to keep it open twenty-four hours a day. The *coyotes* post lookouts to signal when it is safe to transport their *pollos*. Two minutes after the checkpoint closes, vans and trucks that have been parked a few miles south are being loaded up and are on their way to Los Angeles.

The border patrol is familiar with the *coyotes'* strategy. They often know the names of most of the lookouts and what shifts they are working.

Since the border patrol and the illegal aliens are on opposing sides in an ongoing war, there have been some violent confrontations between them. Usually, though, they are friendly enemies. As a border patrol agent takes his busload of illegal aliens to a port of entry where they will walk back across the border into Mexico, he knows that at least half of his prisoners will try to return to the United States within twenty-four hours. "*Adios, amigo,*" the deportees may say to their captor. "Next time, we will be more careful."

"I'll be watching for you," says the border patrol officer with a smile.

In one case, two border patrolmen got their car stuck in the sand on the northern side of the border. "Can you give us a hand?" they called to two Mexican youths standing on the opposite riverbank. Without question, the boys swam across the river, helped the patrolmen out of their predicament, then returned to Mexico.

"I have a lot of respect for the people who come here

looking for work," said one border patrol officer. "What other choice do they have? But still, it's my job to catch as many of them as I can."

The fact is, though, that only one out of every five illegal aliens is caught at the border, and only half of the alarms set off by the border patrol's electronic sensors are responded to. "There are just too many of them [the illegals] and not enough of us," said an immigration official. "Only about thirty miles of our two-thousand-mile border is fenced. To do our job right, there would have to be an officer standing every few feet, twenty-four hours a day, along the entire border."

Once a *sin papeles* is in the United States, there is little chance he will be caught by the immigration service. He may simply take a bus to the nearest city where he will disappear into the crowds, or he may walk to a nearby farming community. In many cases, a *coyote* will have arranged to transport him in a van or a truck or, less often, on a late-night airplane flight to a prearranged job site.

Most immigrants are heading for California, Texas, Arizona, and Florida, but they may end up working in the garment district of New York, the factories of Chicago, or the fields and orchards of Michigan and Oregon.

To most Mexicans, being deported is nothing but an inconvenience. The trip back from their country may be hazardous, but it is one that is easily made again and again. But to Ecuadorans or Hondurans, who may have sold all their possessions and also gone into debt for their trip to the United States, deportation means that they will return home to face even worse poverty than they endured before they left. The fear of *la migra* remains with them every minute they are in this country.

In some cases, this ever-present fear is compounded by the fact that imprisonment or death may await the deportee when he or she returns to his or her homeland. Thousands of Haitians fled to Florida when their lives were threatened by a tyrannical dictator. The unstable governments of some

Central American countries cause citizens to be favored by the rulers one month, only to find that they are objects of persecution the next. Such situations have caused thousands of Guatemalans and Salvadorans to flee to the United States. If they are caught by the INS, they may be able to avoid deportation if they can prove that they are political refugees. Unfortunately, such proof is hard to come by.

After a *sin papeles* enters the United States, he is a stranger in an often hostile land. An unscrupulous[4] employer can easily victimize[5] a desperate man or woman who is willing to take a job no matter how low the pay or how poor the working conditions. Most *sin papeles* are afraid to open a bank account, because to do so means leaving a record of their presence in this country. They are also unwilling to leave their money in their dwelling places because if they are deported, they may not be given time to collect their belongings. As a result, many of them carry large amounts of money in their wallets, making them an attractive target for thieves.

Several illegal immigrants may pool their money to pay a month's rent on an apartment. A dishonest landlord, after collecting his money in advance, may report his tenants to the INS. After their capture, he will repeat the procedure again and again, making many times the profit he would make if he were honest.

An illegal immigrant's fear of *la migra* extends to anyone who wears a uniform or is in any way connected to the government. If he is robbed, he is afraid to report the crime to the police. If he is cheated by an employer, a landlord, or a merchant, he is afraid to file a complaint with the proper agency. If he needs medical help, he hesitates to seek treatment from a doctor or a hospital.

---

[4] dishonest; without conscience or principles

[5] swindle; cheat; cause to suffer

Most *sin papeles* come from a culture where family ties are supremely important, and all but a few of them must leave their families behind. As months turn into years of separation, the emotional pain they suffer is tremendous.

These and many other factors combine to overwhelm the *sin papeles* as they try to cope with life in *El Norte*. Fortunately, their plight is eased by many churches, social service agencies, and volunteer groups that give counseling, legal advice, food, and shelter to thousands of illegal aliens every day. This help may represent the only support the immigrants receive as they strive for a better life.

To the *sin papeles*, the hope of getting a job in the United States far outweighs any possible problems they may face. As long as the situation in their homelands is hopeless, they will continue to seek work in *El Norte*.

It's estimated that there are one to three million illegal aliens in the United States at any one time. Many citizens object to this situation.

"They're taking away jobs that belong to us," says an unemployed mechanic.

The fact is that most undocumented, or illegal, workers have only a second-grade education and very few job skills. As a result, they are happy to take the jobs that most Americans don't want or will take only temporarily. Farmers, restaurant owners, and clothing manufacturers would have a difficult time staying in business without the *sin papeles*. Some economists have gone so far as to say that the economy of some states—California, for one—would grind to a halt if all of the undocumented workers suddenly disappeared.

"Illegal aliens don't pay their fair share of taxes," says a grocery store clerk.

Like many American citizens who are unable to find full-time employment, illegal aliens are often paid in cash by people who hire them for gardening or paving a driveway or building a wall. Those who have found more permanent jobs, however, have federal, state, and other taxes deducted from their checks. The big difference between them and the legal residents is that most illegal aliens probably won't be in this country long enough to collect any overpayment on their income tax or to reap any benefits from the money they have contributed to Social Security.

"But their children are going to school here," a mother of three complains. "Aren't we paying for their education?"

Only a small percentage of *sin papeles* bring their children with them. Also, any illegal alien who lives in a house or an apartment pays rent, part of which is used for the landlord's property taxes, which support our schools. One problem that does arise wherever there are non-English-speaking children attending school is that of communication. Many classes in the Los Angeles, California, school system must be conducted in both English and Spanish. This bilingual education costs more than teaching in only one language.

"Illegal aliens send most of their money home," says the owner of a market. "Since they don't spend it here, our own business people are suffering."

It's true that undocumented workers send a large share of their wages to their families back home. It's also true that hundreds of clothing stores, markets, and places of entertainment have come into existence just to serve the needs of the great numbers of Hispanic and Caribbean immigrants. These businesses contribute to the economic health of their communities. Still, many economists issue warnings about the dangers of a "money drain" from the United States into foreign countries.

"If all these foreigners keep coming, someday they will outnumber us," says a retired army officer.

Many people are concerned about the fact that the number of immigrants, both legal and illegal, has increased dramatically during the past twenty years. Some of them resent having any language but English used in our schools and businesses and polling places. They are frightened at the changes that people from other cultures have brought with them.

But, reply historians, almost all of our not too distant ancestors came from somewhere else. Our current society is a result of the blending of these many diverse cultures. Eventually, as in the past, "they," the immigrants we fear today, will be absorbed into our communities and will become "us," accepted members of our society.

Sin papeles know little about the problems or benefits they bring to the United States. As long as there are no jobs in their countries and there is work to be found here, they will continue to cross our border, and the INS will continue to do everything in its power to catch them. To offset a lack of money and manpower, our immigration officials consider any idea that may help them do their job more efficiently. One suggestion has been to build a wall along our entire southern border. It was decided that such a structure would be too expensive to construct and to maintain.

The busiest illegal alien entry point is located just a few miles south of San Diego, California. Recently, a string of powerful floodlights was erected on the levees along that portion of the border. Few *sin papeles* have been deterred.[6] They simply cross outside the circle of illumination.

Several years ago, someone suggested that a deep, wide ditch be dug just north of the border running in an eastwest direction across the California-Arizona deserts. This idea was never seriously considered. Besides doing damage to the fragile ecology of that area, the project would be very expensive.

The Immigration Reform and Control Act of 1986 was the most far-reaching plan ever put into effect to stem the flow of illegal aliens into the United States. One aim of the program was to give millions of undocumented workers who were already established here the chance to apply for amnesty[7] and be free of the fear of deportation. Eventually,

---

[6] prevented or discouraged from acting

after learning basic English and taking courses in United States history and government, they could become legal residents and even citizens.

The second aim was to make it impossible for illegal aliens to find jobs. This goal was to be accomplished by punishing the employers who hired undocumented workers.

For over two years after the amnesty program went into effect, there was a decrease in the number of people illegally entering our country. Then, as amnesty applicants became temporary legal residents, many of them sent for their families. Also, many *sin papeles* bought false papers and presented them to their prospective employers. Since the employers weren't required to verify the papers, undocumented workers were still being hired.

By 1990 there were just as many people entering our country illegally as there had been before 1986. It had become evident that the amnesty law was a failure. There was talk of hiring more border patrol officers and of supplying them with more helicopters, planes, jeeps, and horses; of putting up more walls and fences; and of installing more lights. The problem with all of these measures, though, is that they don't change the fact that the United States is an irresistible magnet to the poverty-stricken people south of our border.

"They will continue to come, no matter what," said the administrator of a migrant shelter in Tijuana, Mexico. "The United States could build a moat and fill it with sharks and crocodiles, but they will still find a way to cross the border."

Some of our own government officials agree that any attempt to keep out the *sin papeles* is doomed to failure, that the holes in our leaky southern border can never be effectively plugged. They are in favor of having an open border, over which people can come and go at will.

---

[7] the act of a government by which pardon is granted to a whole class of persons

"We need the workers, and the workers need us," they argue. "Don't punish them just for trying to earn a living."

The *sin papeles* know they are breaking the law when they enter the United States illegally. The fact that they are considered criminals, however, is unimportant compared to the fact that *El Norte* represents their only hope of survival. They must work or their families will starve.

REVIEWING AND INTERPRETING

Record your answers to these questions in your personal literature notebook. Follow the directions for each part.

REVIEWING Try to complete each of these sentences without looking back at the selection.

Recalling Facts **1.** Most of the people who enter the United States are from
  a. El Salvador.
  b. Cuba.
  c. Colombia.
  d. Mexico.

Understanding Main Ideas **2.** According to the author, most aliens come to the United States
  a. as political refugees.
  b. for the medical benefits.
  c. to take jobs from American citizens.
  d. to support their families.

Identifying Sequence **3.** The United States Immigration and Naturalization Service (INS) was created
  a. during the 1800s.
  b. when amnesty was granted to all illegal aliens.
  c. when laws were passed to control the number of aliens who were allowed to become legal residents.
  d. after the Immigration Reform and Control Act of 1986 was passed.

Finding Supporting Details **4.** As an example of the border patrol's ineffectiveness, Poynter
  a. describes how easy it is for Mexicans to cross the border.
  b. gives details about the Immigration Reform and Control Act of 1986.
  c. describes how employers are punished for hiring aliens.
  d. says that the amnesty law was a failure.

Getting Meaning from Context

5. "However, the possibility of dealing with a dishonest *coyote* is the first hazard many illegal aliens must face." The word *hazard* means

  a. person.
  b. decision.
  c. danger.
  d. job.

INTERPRETING   To complete these items, you may look back at the selection if you'd like.

Making Inferences

6. From this essay you can infer that Poynter

  a. believes the government should give more money to the border patrol.
  b. resents having any language other than English used in schools.
  c. disagrees with those who want to stop immigration to the United States.
  d. thinks all schools should offer bilingual education.

Generalizing

7. In this essay Poynter supports her argument mostly with

  a. personal experience.
  b. facts, examples, and description.
  c. in-depth interviews.
  d. statistics.

Recognizing Fact and Opinion

8. According to the essay, which of the following is a statement of fact?

  a. In 1986 illegal aliens could apply for amnesty.
  b. The emotional pain the aliens suffer is tremendous.
  c. The jobs aliens find in the United States are dreams come true.
  d. To most Mexicans, being deported is nothing but an inconvenience.

Identifying Cause and Effect

9. Because the United States border is not completely protected,

    a. the punishment for illegally entering the country is severe.

    b. deported aliens often return within 24 hours.

    c. the United States government ignores the problem of illegal aliens.

    d. *coyotes* take advantage of their clients.

Drawing Conclusions

10. From the essay you can conclude that

    a. illegal aliens cost United States citizens millions of dollars.

    b. it is difficult to find a solution for the problem of illegal aliens.

    c. illegal aliens pay local and federal taxes.

    d. Americans should build a ditch along the border.

Now check your answers with your teacher. Study the items you answered incorrectly. What skills are they checking? Talk with your teacher about ways to work on those skills.

The Persuasive Essay

An *essay* is a brief work of nonfiction that expresses a person's opinion or view about a particular subject. The purpose of an essay may be to express ideas or feelings, to analyze a topic, to inform, to entertain, or to persuade. Often, an essayist, a person who writes essays, tries to persuade readers to accept his or her view about a given subject. The word *essay*, in fact, comes from the French word *essai*, which means "to try."

Before accepting the opinion of the author of a persuasive essay about a subject, it is important to evaluate what he or she says. *Evaluating* is the process of judging the merit, or worth, of the facts and opinions that an author presents. We actually evaluate people or events every day. We can tell whether someone is in a good or bad mood by evaluating his or her words or actions. When we read a book or see a movie, we can usually tell why we liked or disliked it. Without always being aware of it, we are constantly analyzing and evaluating.

There are many elements to consider when you evaluate a persuasive essay. In the lessons that follow, we will talk about three of those elements:

1. **Identifying Opinions** When authors write persuasive essays, they try to convince readers that their opinions are correct. You remember that an *opinion* is a statement of what someone thinks, not a view that can be proved or disproved. As you read, try to identify the author's opinions. Then decide whether you agree or disagree with those opinions.

2. **Identifying Support for an Opinion** An opinion by itself cannot convince someone to think a certain way. To persuade readers, an author supports his or her opinion with specific information. Evaluate the information the author uses to support an opinion. Ask yourself whether you agree with or believe that supporting information.

3. **Identifying Loaded Language** An author of a persuasive essay usually uses words or phrases that appeal to the emotions. Such loaded language is intended to produce a positive or negative feeling about what the author is describing.

LESSON ① IDENTIFYING OPINIONS

There are four basic types of nonfiction writing. *Narration* gives the events and actions of a story, as in Robert Silverberg's "Pompeii: A Snapshot in Time." *Description* helps readers to picture a person, a place, or an event. *Exposition* presents information, as in Becky Rupp's "The Icing of the Cream." *Persuasion* is an attempt to persuade readers to accept an opinion. In persuasive essays, writers often use arguments to convince readers that their opinions are correct.

When you think of the word *argument*, you may think of people strongly disagreeing with one another. The word has another meaning, however. *Argument* can also mean the persuasive reasoning a writer uses to lead the reader to a logical conclusion. Although you may not be aware of it, you see *argumentation* in persuasive writing all the time. Political candidates running for office send out leaflets presenting arguments to convince citizens to vote for them. Arguments appear in a newspaper's editorial page and on television. Loggers, for example, may try to convince people that it is all right to cut down trees, whereas environmentalists argue that doing so endangers wildlife.

"Sin Papeles" is an example of a writer using arguments to persuade. Poynter's persuasive essay presents a very personal view, so it is filled with her opinions. She believes that the United States should open its borders so that people can come and go at will. This opinion becomes the main idea of her argument. Another point she argues is that illegal aliens are not harming Americans or their way of life and are not costing the government extra money.

When you read a persuasive essay, you should always try to be objective. That is, try to set aside your own biases or prejudices about the author's subject and viewpoint. As you read a persuasive essay, carefully weigh all the evidence, facts, and opinions that the author presents. Then ask yourself: Do I believe the facts? Do the author's opinions make sense to me? Does the author appeal to my emotions but fail to provide supporting facts and other evidence?

The first step in evaluating an essay is to identify the author's opinions. That may sound easy, because opinions are obvious, aren't they? They are if the author says "I think" or "I believe." Opinions are also obvious if they include signal words such as *happy, sad, beautiful,* and *wonderful.* Words that describe how a person feels always signal an opinion.

More often, however, opinions are not so obvious or easy to identify. Many writers state an opinion as if it were a fact. When they do, they are usually not trying to trick you. Most writers simply assume that you can distinguish between facts and opinions.

Read this passage from the essay and see whether you can identify the sentence that states an opinion.

> They come from such impoverished countries as Mexico, Guatemala, Colombia, and Haiti, where at least half of them live in dirt-floored hovels with no plumbing or electricity. Only a few understand English; most of them can't read or write their native language. The jobs they find here are dreams come true.

Did you find the sentence that states the author's opinion? Look closely. Poynter gives readers many facts: the countries she lists are poor; most immigrants from those countries don't understand English; they can't read or write their native languages. These are *facts*—statements that can be proved or disproved. But the last sentence is an opinion. You cannot prove that the immigrants feel that the jobs are dreams come true.

Perhaps many hate the jobs they are able to find. Yet the author states her opinion as if it were a fact. She feels that she is drawing a logical conclusion from the facts she has presented. Poynter is using facts to convince you that her opinion is correct.

EXERCISE ①

Read this passage from the essay. Use what you have learned in this lesson to answer the questions that follow it.

> The fact is that most undocumented, or illegal, workers have only a second-grade education and very few job skills. As a result, they are happy to take the jobs that most Americans don't want or will take only temporarily. Farmers, restaurant owners, and clothing manufacturers would have a difficult time staying in business without the *sin papeles*. Some economists have gone so far as to say that the economy of some states—California, for one—would grind to a halt if all of the undocumented workers suddenly disappeared.

1. What sentence in the passage expresses the author's opinion? Is it clearly stated as an opinion, or does it appear as a statement of fact?

2. What two facts does the author include in the passage?

Now check your answers with your teacher. Review this lesson if you don't understand why an answer was incorrect.

WRITING ON YOUR OWN ①

In this exercise you will use what you learned in this lesson to explore your opinions and choose the one that will be the focus of your argument. Follow these steps:

- Review the list you wrote for Writing: Developing a Persuasive Essay. Choose one of the issues from your list. Write down your opinion about the issue you chose. For example, if you chose "save the environment," you might state your opinion like this: "People are not concerned enough about the environment. They should be doing all that they can to improve and protect it."
- Make a list of examples, or reasons, that support your opinion. If, for example, you were writing about the environment, you might use the following examples: "people pollute our groundwater by using chemical fertilizers on their lawns; they pollute our air by not carpooling; they add to air and water pollution by refusing to recycle metal, glass, and plastic."
- Reread the list of examples that support your opinion. Could you add other examples to the list that might help convince your readers that your opinion is correct?

LESSON ② IDENTIFYING SUPPORT FOR AN OPINION

Suppose you believe that recycling is a great idea, and you choose this as the opinion you want to argue in your essay. If you wanted to convince your friends that they also should recycle, the first step would be to support your opinion. If you present logical arguments, you may find that your friends agree with you. You could talk about how less and less land is available for landfills; to conserve land, therefore, people should recycle. You could explain how pollution can be reduced by recycling plastic instead of making new plastic. In this way you would be using facts to support your opinion.

Poynter uses several techniques to support her opinions. We will examine three of them: facts, quoting sources, and generalizations.

Facts In "Sin Papeles" Poynter supports her opinions about illegal aliens by using facts. Read this passage from the essay.

The Immigration Reform and Control Act of 1986 was the most far-reaching plan ever put into effect to stem the flow of illegal aliens into the United States. One aim of the program was to give millions of undocumented workers who were already established here the chance to apply for amnesty and be free of the fear of deportation. Eventually, after learning basic English and taking courses in United States history and government, they could become legal residents and even citizens. . . .

By 1990 there were just as many people entering our country illegally as there had been before 1986. It had become evident that the amnesty law was a failure.

You can easily check the facts Poynter presents in that passage to see whether they are true. An encyclopedia contains information about the aims of the Immigration Reform and Control Act of 1986. It tells how the law failed to prevent illegal aliens from entering the country. Facts help to make the author's opinions believable.

Quoting Sources Writers also support their opinions by using statements made by someone in authority. Quoting experts and other reliable sources is a very effective way of supporting an opinion. Quotations help convince readers that they can believe what the author is saying. Read the following passage. Why do you think Poynter chose to quote government officials?

Some of our own government officials agree that any attempt to keep out the *sin papeles* is doomed to failure, that the holes in our leaky southern border can never be effectively plugged. They are in favor of having an open border, over which people can come and go at will.

"We need the workers, and the workers need us," they argue. "Don't punish them just for trying to earn a living."

The quotation supports Poynter's opinion that the United States should have an open border. She points out that even government officials agree that we need to change our immigration policies and that illegal aliens want only to work. You may agree with Poynter, but remember to evaluate what she writes. In this quotation she has chosen to cite only those officials who *agree* with her point of view. What do those who *disagree* say?

Generalizations   Another effective method Poynter uses is to point out the opposition's use of unsupported generalizations. A *generalization* is a broad statement or conclusion that is true for *some* or *most*—but not *all* examples. For example, the statement "Most people who graduate from college earn more money in their lifetime than those who don't graduate from college" is a generalization. The statement "People who graduate from college are happier than those who do not graduate from college" is also a generalization. It is not a valid generalization, however, because it cannot be supported by reliable facts. Generalizations are often signaled by clue words such as *all*, *most*, *many*, *few*, *sometimes*, and *always*. The first example presented of a generalization is signaled by the word *most*. The second example has no signal word. Watch for generalizations when you read. When you recognize a statement as a generalization, evaluate it to see whether it is supported by facts. If it is, it's a valid generalization.

In the following sentences from the essay, Poynter points out unsupported generalizations made by people who oppose her opinion.

> "Illegal aliens don't pay their fair share of taxes," says a grocery clerk.
> "Illegal aliens send most their money home," says the owner of a market. "Because they don't spend it here, our own business people are suffering."

No additional information shows whether the clerk and the owner of the market have supported their generalizations with facts. Poynter quotes their unsupported generalizations and then argues against them by presenting the facts. She says that some illegal aliens do find jobs at which state, federal, and other taxes are deducted from their paychecks. She then goes on to say that they won't be in the country long enough to collect any overpayment on their income tax or collect any Social Security benefits. It is usually easy to spot generalizations that are not supported by facts. Could Poynter argue as successfully against statements supported by specific examples or details?

EXERCISE ②

Use what you have learned in this lesson to answer these questions.

1. What techniques does Poynter use to support her opinions in these two sentences from the essay?
   a. "They're taking away jobs that belong to us," says an unemployed mechanic.
   b. Before the start of the twentieth century, there was no such thing as an illegal alien in the United States.

2. How can you evaluate each of those statements?

Now check your answers with your teacher. Review this lesson if you don't understand why an answer was incorrect.

 ## WRITING ON YOUR OWN ②

In this exercise you will use what you have learned in this lesson to develop support for your opinion. Follow these steps:

- Reread the list of examples you wrote for Writing on Your Own 1. Think about what you have learned in the lesson about how an author supports opinions. Poynter supports her opinions with facts, quotations from witnesses, and generalizations.
- Using your list of examples, write two or three paragraphs adding facts, quotations, and generalizations to your examples. Read the following sample paragraph to see how you can work these techniques into your writing:

> People are not concerned about the environment. They should be doing all that they can to improve and protect it. (opinion) The Environmental Protection Agency is trying to reduce air and water pollution. (fact) It's not an easy task, however. People are polluters. (generalization) One marine biologist has said, "Pollution is so bad that there is a manmade oil slick over the entire ocean's surface." (quotation)

LESSON ③   IDENTIFYING LOADED LANGUAGE

Authors often use loaded language to persuade readers to think a certain way or to accept their opinions. *Loaded language* is made up of words and phrases that appeal to the emotions—for example: "I'll never work at Slater's Store again. My irresponsible boss threatens to fire me if I'm late. The other workers are lazy, and I get stuck doing all the dirty work." How many examples of loaded language can you find in those three sentences? Look at the words the writer uses to create a negative feeling about Slater's: *irresponsible*, *lazy*, *stuck*, and *dirty*. The writer is trying to convince readers that he or she has good reasons for never working at Slater's again. Writers use loaded language in their supporting details to strengthen their arguments.

When you evaluate an essay, it is important to look for words or phrases that the author uses to appeal to the emotions in order to give the reader positive or negative feelings about the subject. You may agree with what the writer is saying, but you should realize that he or she is appealing to your emotions. Read this passage from the essay and look for examples of loaded language:

> To get these menial, tedious, low-paying, often physically grueling jobs, these men and women walk, crawl, and swim across our southern border, facing hardships and dangers in the darkness of night. They come from . . . impoverished countries . . . where at least half of them live in dirt-floored hovels with no plumbing or electricity.

Poynter doesn't say the jobs are paid at the minimum-wage level or that they are boring. Instead she uses words that make you feel sorry for the illegal aliens: *menial, tedious, low-paying, grueling, crawl, darkness of night, impoverished,* and *dirt-floored hovels.* Imagine if Poynter had written this instead: "To find work, men and women cross the border. They come from poor countries that have a low standard of living." Would you feel as sympathetic toward these men and women if you were not aware of the hardships that they must face? Poynter's choice of words helps support her argument—that these people are desperate to make a living and will face any obstacle to find work.

The author is not trying to trick readers by using loaded language. She is trying to make us feel the same way she feels by appealing to our emotions. Before you can decide whether your emotional response is justified, you must examine how the author has influenced your feelings by the language he or she uses.

EXERCISE ③

Read this passage from the essay. Use what you have learned in this lesson to answer the questions that follow it.

> After a *sin papeles* enters the United States, he is a stranger in an often hostile land. An unscrupulous employer can easily victimize a desperate man or woman who is willing to take a job no matter how low the pay or how poor the working conditions. Most *sin papeles* are afraid to open a bank account, because to do so means leaving a record of their presence in this country. They are also unwilling to leave their money in their dwelling places because if they are deported, they may not be given time to collect their belongings. As a result, many of them carry large amounts of money in their wallets, making them an attractive target for thieves.
>
> Several illegal immigrants may pool their money to pay a month's rent on an apartment. A dishonest landlord, after collecting his money in advance, may report his tenants to the INS.

1. What examples of loaded language do you find in the passage?

2. How does the author's use of loaded language strengthen and support her argument?

Now check your answers with your teacher. Review this lesson if you don't understand why an answer was incorrect.

WRITING ON YOUR OWN ③

In this exercise you will use what you learned in this lesson to add loaded language to your paragraphs to support your argument by appealing to readers' emotions. Follow these steps:

- Reread the paragraphs you wrote for Writing on Your Own 2. What words can you add to your paragraphs that will create positive or negative feelings about your subject? Look again at the sample paragraph from Writing on Your Own 2. Notice the words to which italics have been added:

> People are not concerned about the environment. They should be doing all that they can to improve and protect it. (opinion) The Environmental Protection Agency is *struggling* to reduce air and water pollution. (fact) It's an *overwhelming task*, however. People are polluters. (generalization) One *concerned* marine biologist has said, "Pollution is so bad that there is a manmade oil slick over the entire ocean's surface." (quotation)

- Now rewrite your paragraphs, adding words that appeal to your readers' emotions.

DISCUSSION GUIDES

1. In her essay Poynter says, "The fact is that most undocumented, or illegal, workers have only a second-grade education and very few job skills. As a result, they are happy to take the jobs that most Americans don't want or will take only temporarily." Do you agree that illegal aliens take jobs that most Americans don't want or will take only temporarily? If you agree, explain why you think Americans won't take those jobs. If you disagree, explain your opinion. Organize a class debate to discuss both sides of the issue.

2. As you have learned, Poynter uses many techniques to persuade readers that her opinion is logical and correct. In a small group discuss these questions: Do you agree with Poynter's position? Do you think she uses reasonable examples and facts, or does she appeal more to your emotions than to reason?

3. Some government officials believe we should have an open border between the United States and Mexico. Others feel we should exercise strict controls over who is allowed to cross. Based on what you know and what you've read in this essay, what do you think is the best solution? Present your ideas to the class.

WRITE A PERSUASIVE ESSAY

In this unit you have learned how to develop a persuasive argument. Now you will use that argument to write a persuasive essay.

Follow these steps to complete your essay. If you have any questions about the writing process, refer to Using the Writing Process (page 220).

- Gather and review the following pieces of writing you did in this unit: 1) the list of issues and notes, 2) your opinion statement and list of examples, or reasons, that support your opinion, 3) the paragraphs using facts, quotations, generalizations, and loaded language.
- Make a graphic organizer like the one shown.

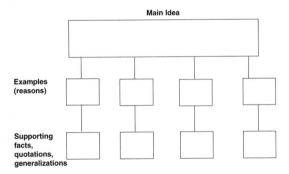

- Using the information and ideas from the paragraphs you've developed, fill in the organizer. Be sure that the examples (reasons) you use support your opinion. And be sure that the facts, quotations, and generalizations you include support the examples.
- Using your graphic organizer as a guide, write a draft of your persuasive essay.
- Review your draft to be sure you've added loaded language to your examples.
- Ask a classmate to read your essay. Ask whether your arguments are convincing. If they are not, ask why they are not. Revise your draft to strengthen and support your arguments.
- Proofread your final draft. Make a clean copy and save it in your writing portfolio.

The Humorous Essay

A Good Deed Goes Wrong

by Patrick McManus

INTRODUCTION

BUILDING BACKGROUND

Nonfiction writing can be serious or humorous. Sometimes writers include humorous incidents or anecdotes in serious works to enliven a story or to make a point. At other times they write humorous pieces solely for the purpose of entertaining. Such is the case with the humorous essay you are about to read, Patrick McManus's "A Good Deed Goes Wrong."

You will recall that an essay is a brief work of nonfiction that deals with a person's opinion or view about a particular subject. Many essays, called personal essays, are based on the personal experiences of the author. In this essay McManus relates some incidents that happened when he was a young boy. In telling the story, he introduces two of the most entertaining characters you will ever meet—his young friend Crazy Eddie Muldoon and Rancid Crabtree, a crotchety old woodsman. Is the story true? Well—we'll let you be the judge of that.

This American bobcat is named for its stubby tail. How would you like to wake up to find this cat looking you in the eye?

Patrick McManus was born in 1933 in Sandpoint, Idaho. He writes a monthly humor column for *Outdoor Life*. He has also written eight books that have humorous themes. Most of his essays are based on personal experience. When asked about humor, McManus says, "There are many standard devices humor writers can use to get laughs, but the best humor arises naturally out of the personalities of the characters in the stories and the comic situation in which they are placed."

More and more young adults have discovered McManus's work. He says, "I direct my humor at a broad audience and have been particularly pleased in recent years to find so many young people reading my books. Many of my stories are based on my own youth, and since everyone was young once, people of all ages seem to identify with the boy Pat and all his weird friends. Apparently, everybody has weird friends."

The lessons that follow "A Good Deed Goes Wrong" focus on some of the techniques used in writing humor.

The author's main purpose in writing this humorous essay is to entertain readers with his version of some events and experiences he recalls from his childhood days. In this unit you will study some of the ways that writers and tellers of humorous stories, such as McManus, make us laugh when we read or hear their stories.

 WRITING: DEVELOPING A HUMOROUS ESSAY

At the end of this unit, you will write a humorous essay describing a humorous event that you or someone you know experienced. The following suggestions will help you get started.

- In a small group discuss humorous events that you or someone you know has experienced. Perhaps you remember your
  parents or grandparents telling you about a comic incident
  that they experienced. Maybe your best friend had a humorous experience. Think about events in your life. Did something funny occur in kindergarten or elementary school? For
  example, did you dress up in a Halloween costume for a
  party at school only to discover that it was the wrong day?
  Did you ever give your dog a bath? (That was probably a
  humorous experience!) Have your brothers or sisters done
  something funny?
- Once you have brainstormed for ideas, list two or three of
  these events that you think are the most humorous.
- Beside each of these events, make some notes giving a brief
  general description of the event.

AS YOU READ   Think about these questions as you read "A Good Deed Goes
Wrong." They will help you identify and understand the
methods that McManus uses to make his essay humorous.

- What scenes in the essay make you laugh? What do you
  think makes those scenes funny?
- Can you picture some of the scenes that McManus
  describes? How do those mental pictures add to the humor
  of the essay?
- Does McManus always mean exactly what he says? When
  does he sometimes mean the opposite of what he says?

A Good Deed Goes Wrong

by Patrick McManus

Some people thought Crazy Eddie Muldoon and I were to blame for breaking Rancid Crabtree's leg. Oddly, the odorous and crotchety old woodsman himself was one of the people who thought this. He said as soon as he got off his crutches he intended to run Eddie and me down and whale the tar out of us. We weren't too worried. We figured by the time Rancid got out of the cast he would have cooled off enough to see that the accident was really his own doing and no fault of ours. But before he got off his crutches, the little incident with the bobcat occurred, generally confusing matters even more. As Crazy Eddie observed at the time, you try to do a kind deed for a person, and it just gets you into more trouble. Anyway, here are the true facts about the entire mess.

During our Christmas vacation from third grade, Eddie and I built a toboggan run up on the mountain behind Rancid's shack. The design of our run was based on one we had seen in newsreels at the Pandora Theater the Saturday before. The two runs were almost identical, except ours was steeper and faster than the one in the newsreel, and went over and under logs and had brush on both sides of it, and at least one of the turns was much sharper, and if you didn't make that turn you would be shot off into space and sail for some time over the valley looking down at the tiny cows and cars beneath you, and this in turn might elevate your anxiety to a dangerous level. So you wanted to be sure to make that sharp curve.

We built the first part of the run on an old logging road that zigzagged down the mountain. We tramped up and down the road the distance of two switchbacks,[1] packing down the snow into a track slightly wider than the width of our sled. The grade on the switchbacks was modest, but sufficient to build up a fair head of speed in a sled by the time it and its driver reached the curve at the end of the second switchback. Then came the good part. Instead of curving the track onto the next switchback, we funneled it over the edge of the road into an old skid trail.

The skid trail had been gouged into the mountains by old-time loggers dragging logs down it. In fact, it was so steep they probably didn't have to drag the logs but merely had to roll them into it and let them shoot to the bottom of the mountain. Erosion had cut the trail down to bare rock, which was now coated with ice, making it even better for a toboggan run. When we were building up our curved bank to funnel the track into the skid trail, Eddie slipped and nearly shot down the run with nothing but his body, and would have if he hadn't managed to grab a small tree and pull himself back up.

"Wow!" he said. "This is going to be good!"

At the bottom end, the skid trail intersected[2] with the next switchback of the road. This was where the toboggan driver would shoot off into space if he failed to make the turn onto the switchback. Fortunately, there was a high bank on the downhill side of the road, only slightly offset from the track. The driver would have to be alert enough to steer toward the high bank, which would sweep the sled up and around and then redirect it back down onto the switchback.

---

[1] zigzag roads or trails for climbing a steep hill

[2] overlapped; met or crossed at a point

This was the last switchback and it provided a straightaway that, at the bottom, merged with the Sand Creek Road. The straightaway was quite steep, so the toboggan driver wouldn't have to worry about his speed diminishing[3] any when he hit this last stretch. He could then glide to a gradual stop on the Sand Creek road, which was seldom traveled during winter, and even then only by old Mrs. Swisher, who drove to church on it each Sunday. We completed the track on a Friday and planned to make our first test run on Saturday.

The next morning, Crazy Eddie and I were dragging my sled past Rancid's shack on our way up to test our toboggan run and were arguing about who got to go down it first.

"Listen, Eddie, it's my sled!" I said.

"Yeah, that's right," he replied. "That's why you should get to be first to test the run."

"No sirree," I said. "I should be the one who gets to choose who goes first, and I choose you."

About then Rancid stuck his head out the door of his shack. "What you boys up to now?" he hollered at us. "Some kinder monkey bidness, no doubt. Ah ain't never seen no younguns what could get into more trouble than you two."

"We built a toboggan run up on the mountain, just like in the newsreel, Rancid. It's fast too."

"Hold up a sec," he said, putting on his coat. "Ah better go check this out. You fool half-pints probably invented some new way to kill yersevs."

Half an hour later, we stood at the start of the toboggan run, all of us still puffing great clouds of vapor from the climb up the trail.

Rancid stared at the little track going down the first switchback. It didn't look nearly so impressive this morning. "Shoot," he said, chuckling. "You call this a toboggan run? Ah cain't believe Ah clumb all the way up hyar to see this piddlin' little trail in the snow. Ah must hev been outta maw

---

[3] lessening; slowing down

mind. Gimme thet sled. The least you can do is let me ride back to the bottom of the mountain on it."

I handed over the sled. Rancid plopped down on it, sitting upright with his long legs sticking way out in front, his coat completely concealing the sled beneath him.

"It might be dangerous, Mr. Crabtree," Eddie warned.

"Dangerous!" Rancid said. "Eddie, Ah 'spect Ah never told you, but Ah used to be a professional bobsledder, jist like you see in the movies. Racin' Rancid they use to call me."

"Gee," I said. "I didn't know that." I figured that he must have been a professional bobsledder right after being a fighter pilot and before he became a big-game hunter in Africa or about the same time he was a champion prizefighter.

"Yep," Rancid said, poking a wad of chewing tobacco into his cheek. "Now gimme a shove off."

He glided slowly away toward the first curve, gradually picking up speed. He called back to us as he went around the curve. "Ah hate to tell you this, boys, but your bobsled track ain't steep enough even to give a feller a decent ride."

We were disappointed in the professional bobsledder's assessment of our run but thought his opinion of it might improve later on. Sure enough, the next time we heard him yell was about when we thought he should hit the funnel into the skid trail.

"GOL-DAAAAAAA-A-A-A-a-a-n-n-n-n-g-g-g-g!"

"I think he liked the skid-trail section," Eddie said.

"Yeah," I said. "He sounded excited."

So that is how Rancid broke his leg. He said later he didn't know when, where, or how he broke his leg, or even that he had, because his mind was so occupied with other matters, among which was whaling the tar out of Eddie and me at the first opportunity.

The only eyewitness other than Rancid was old Mrs. Swisher, who was a little daft anyway and really couldn't be relied on for an accurate observation. "I got a little mixed up," she related, "and thinking it was Sunday instead of

Saturday, I started driving to town to go to church. As always, I was especially nervous going by that dreadful Rancid Crabtree's shack, because he's in cahoots with the devil. Well, I'm driving along real careful minding my own business when all of sudden that fool Crabtree zooms right by me, just flying he was, about a foot in the air, going like the wind. I just caught a glimpse of his face, he was going so fast, and I'm sorry I did, because it had such a hideous expression on it you can't even imagine! The thought of it has kept me awake nights ever since. And he's holding this little green tree in one hand, torn right out by the roots it was. I bet the tree had something to do with one of those devilish rites of his. Well, he shot off down Sand Creek Hill, and I thought he might be laying in ambush for me up ahead, so I turned right around and went home, and it was a good thing I did, too, because then I remembered it was Saturday instead of Sunday."

Naturally, nobody took daft old Mrs. Swisher's account seriously, although Eddie and I did recover my sled at the bottom of Sand Creek Hill, where it had shot off over the bank and landed on the frozen creek. Sprayed out in front of it was what we first thought to be blood but then discovered was nothing more interesting than tobacco juice.

A couple of Saturdays later, Eddie and I were walking along the highway pulling my sled, the runners of which were somewhat splayed[4] out but still worked. We had been trying to come up with an idea for making amends with Rancid, when we saw a furry shape lying on the highway. Both of us had fine roadkill collections and this specimen looked exceptional.

"It's mine," I said as we rushed forward. "You got the last one."

"No sirree," Eddie said. "I remember. You got that nice flattened toad last fall and . . . Hey, what is this, anyway?"

---

[4] spread out in an awkward manner

"My gosh, it's a bobcat. Feel it. It must have just been killed. It's still warm. Look, it's got a bit of blood on its head where the car hit it, but otherwise it's in great shape. Well, I'd better take my bobcat home. Maybe I'll stuff it."

"No you won't," Eddie said. "I'm gonna take it home and stuff it."

"Hey, wait a minute," I said. "I know what. We'll give it to Rancid. He can skin it and sell the hide. Then he won't be mad at us anymore. What do you say, Eddie?"

Eddie reluctantly agreed. We loaded the bobcat on my sled and hauled it over to Rancid's shack. I pushed the door gently open and peeked inside, to make sure Rancid wasn't close enough to swat me before he saw we had brought him a gift. The old woodsman was still in bed, snoring loudly, his casted foot sticking out from under the covers and resting on a block of firewood. He had pulled a red wool stocking cap over his bare foot where it stuck out of the cast.

"Rancid's still asleep," I whispered to Eddie. "Should we wake him up?"

Crazy Eddie grinned. "Naw, he's probably all pooped out from dragging that cast around with him. Let's just carry the bobcat in and put it on the table next to his bed, so he can see it when he first wakes up. It'll be a nice surprise for him."

Eddie was very good at thinking up nice surprises for people. We carried the bobcat in and laid it down on the table next to the snoring Rancid. Eddie studied the arrangement.

"No good," he whispered. "It looks too dead." He looked around and found a box of kitchen matches. Then he took out two of the matches and used them to prop apart the big cat's lips in a pretty fair imitation of a snarl. Then he stuck the matchbox under the animal's chin so it looked as if the bobcat were holding its head up, ready to spring. Then we tiptoed out and hunkered[5] alongside the door to await the old woodsman's awakening.

---

[5] crouched down

"I think he's gonna be real surprised," Eddie said.

"Yeah, me too."

Presently, Rancid stopped snoring. He muttered something in his sleep. Then he apparently banged the table with his arm, because we heard a bump and then the sound of the matchbox hitting the floor.

"Darn," Eddie whispered. "The matchbox fell out from under the bobcat's chin. The surprise is ruined now."

"Whazzat?" Rancid mumbled. "What in tarnation . . . ? GOL-DANG! GIT! GIT AWAY FROM MEEEE!"

Eddie and I chuckled.

The table crashed to the floor. A chair was flung against the wall and a block of firewood sailed out the door. All of this was accompanied by a terrible roaring and snarling and the wildest cussing I had ever heard.

"GIT BACK! GIT BACK!" Rancid yelled amid all the bangs and crashes and thumps.

Eddie looked at me. "I didn't think he'd be this surprised."

"No fooling," I said nervously. "Maybe we'd better leave right now. We can tell him later about our present for him, when he isn't so surprised."

At that moment there was a furious rattling of crutches and Rancid burst out of the cabin, shot across the yard and into his privy, slamming the door shut behind him.

Eddie and I were so startled we couldn't move. Then the bobcat walked out the door, chewing on a matchstick. It gave us a contemptuous[6] glance and went off up the mountain shaking its head, either because it had a headache or because it couldn't believe what it had just witnessed.

Rancid opened the privy door a crack and watched the bobcat until it disappeared in the woods. Then he saw us. Crazy Eddie and I started toward home.

"You ever seen Rancid move that fast before?" Eddie asked.

---

[6] expressing feelings of scorn or lack of respect

"Nope," I said, glancing back over my shoulder. "'Specially not on crutches."

"Didn't even use his legs," Eddie said, with a touch of awe. "Had those ol' crutches whippin' around like spokes on a wheel. Do you think he was ever an acrobat in a circus?"

"Probably."

"I see he don't sleep in pajamas neither," Eddie said, puffing clouds of vapor into the icy air.

"Yeah," I said, panting my own clouds of vapor. "He probably will after this, though."

We passed daft old Mrs. Swisher's car askew[7] on the road below Rancid's shack. She was staring vacantly at us, her mouth hanging open.

"It's Saturday, Mrs. Swisher," Eddie yelled as we sped past. "Sunday ain't till tomorrow."

She didn't reply. But I could tell she was going to have trouble getting to sleep again that night. It isn't often you see a naked man on crutches with a red stocking cap on his foot chase two boys through the snow on a cold winter morning. What was even stranger, the crippled old woodsman kept gaining on us.

---

[7] out of proper position; turned the wrong way

REVIEWING AND INTERPRETING

Record your answers to these comprehension questions in your personal literature notebook. Follow the directions for each part.

REVIEWING

Try to complete each of these sentences without looking back at the selection.

Recalling Facts

1. When Rancid first saw the sled run, he thought that
   a. it was too dangerous for the boys.
   b. the boys had done a great job.
   c. it was not very impressive.
   d. he should help the boys build a better one.

Understanding Main Ideas

2. The main idea of the essay is that the boys
   a. hated Rancid and planned to trick him.
   b. planned to make the best sled run possible.
   c. didn't plan to cause Rancid so much trouble.
   d. planned to shock Mrs. Swisher.

Identifying Sequence

3. The boys put the bobcat in Rancid's shack
   a. before they built the sled run.
   b. after Rancid broke his leg.
   c. before Rancid made the trip down the trail.
   d. before Rancid broke his leg.

Finding Supporting Details

4. Rancid changed his opinion of the "piddlin' little trail" when he
   a. started down the trail.
   b. saw the trail from the top of the mountain.
   c. got to the bottom of the run.
   d. hit the funnel into the skid trail.

Getting Meaning from Context

5. "She was staring vacantly at us, her mouth hanging open."
The word *vacantly* means
a. with curiosity.
b. without fear.
c. with confidence.
d. without thought.

INTERPRETING To complete these items, you may look back at the selection if you'd like.

Making Inferences

6. You can infer that Rancid
a. admired the two boys.
b. was never a bobsledder.
c. was once a fighter pilot.
d. expected the sled run to be dangerous.

Generalizing

7. Rancid's attitude toward the boys can best be described as
a. angry.
b. disappointed.
c. protective.
d. understanding.

Recognizing Fact and Opinion

8. According to the essay, which of the following statements is an opinion?
a. "We built the first part of the run on an old logging road that zigzagged down the mountain."
b. "I see he don't sleep in pajamas neither."
c. "The skid trail had been gouged into the mountains by old-time loggers dragging logs down it."
d. "I could tell that she was going to have trouble getting to sleep again that night."

Identifying Cause and Effect

9. The boys probably felt that Mrs. Swisher was a little daft because she

    a. didn't like Rancid Crabtree.

    b. drove her car so slowly.

    c. confused Saturday with Sunday.

    d. drove her car off the road.

Drawing Conclusions

10. Eddie probably felt that doing good deeds only got him into more trouble because

    a. Rancid was a professional bobsledder.

    b. Rancid became even more angry.

    c. he wanted to keep the bobcat for himself.

    d. Rancid didn't like the sled run.

Now check your answers with your teacher. Study the questions you answered incorrectly. Whats skills are they checking? Talk to your teacher about ways to work on those skills.

The Humorous Essay

As you read "A Good Deed Goes Wrong," did you wonder how much of the essay was true? Is Rancid Crabtree a real person or is he a character based on someone the author knew when he was a young boy? McManus and his friend Crazy Eddie probably did build a toboggan run. Do you think that it was really as dangerous as McManus describes?

Even though nonfiction is supposed to give factual information about real people, places, and events, humorists—writers and tellers of humorous stories—sometimes cross the dividing line between nonfiction and fiction. As McManus says, "If I stick to the unblemished truth for too long a stretch, I tend to tense up, get a headache."

You can assume that parts of McManus's essay are true. He has had some of these experiences and knows some of these people. But you can also assume that the author added his own humorous insights to the story.

You may have noticed that some people seem to have a gift for telling funny stories and for making people laugh. Other people can tell a story about a very comic event, but it doesn't seem funny. The difference between the two types of storytellers lies in their methods and attitudes.

There are many elements that combine to make a humorous essay. In this unit we will talk about four of those elements:

1. **Exaggeration**   To a writer of humor, facts are not always the most important part of a story. A humorist often overstates, or exaggerates, a fact to add humor to the situation.

2. **Descriptive Language** and **Foreshadowing**   A humorist carefully chooses descriptive words to create a humorous mental picture of an event or an action. He or she may also give a hint or clue about events that are going to happen later in the story. This technique is called *foreshadowing*.

3. **Irony**   Sometimes a humorist says one thing but obviously means just the opposite. The difference between what we expect to happen and what really happens can be very humorous.

LESSON ①   EXAGGERATION

In this book you have studied how nonfiction writers use facts. You have also learned how to determine whether a statement is true. Many writers of nonfiction humor think that the "plain facts" are not always the most important part of a narration, or story. To add humor to their writing they may alter the facts a bit. One common technique for such altering is exaggeration. As you learned in Unit 5 while studying hyperbole, *exaggeration* is an intentional overstatement of facts or events so as to intensify their meanings. When a writer uses exaggeration, he or she is not trying to deceive the reader but to heighten the humor of the situation or the characters he or she is describing.

McManus intentionally uses exaggeration in the following passage to create a humorous mental picture. As you read it, note how he describes what happens if the driver misses a turn on the run.

During our Christmas vacation from third grade, Eddie and I built a toboggan run up on the mountain behind Rancid's shack. The design of our run was based on one we had seen in newsreels at the Pandora Theater the Saturday before. The two runs were almost identical, except ours was steeper and faster than the one in the newsreel, and went over and under logs and had brush on both sides of it, and at least one of the turns was much sharper, and if you didn't make that turn you would be shot off into space and sail for some time over the valley looking down at the tiny cows and cars beneath you, and this in turn might elevate your anxiety to a dangerous level. So you wanted to be sure to make that sharp curve.

Did you find the exaggeration? Think about how high off the ground you would have to be to "sail over the valley looking down at the tiny cows and cars beneath you." McManus has exaggerated what would happen if someone didn't make the turn, to emphasize the idea that the boys' tobaggan run is very steep, very high, and very dangerous. The exaggeration also creates a humorous image. Can you picture in your mind a sled and its driver being "shot off into space"?

EXERCISE ①
Read the following passage from the essay. Use what you have learned in this lesson to answer the questions that follow it.

Eddie and I were so startled we couldn't move. Then the bobcat walked out the door, chewing on a matchstick. It gave us a contemptuous glance and went off up the mountain shaking its head, either because it had a headache or because it couldn't believe what it had just witnessed.

Rancid opened the privy door a crack and watched the bobcat until it disappeared in the woods. Then he saw us. Crazy Eddie and I started toward home.

"You ever seen Rancid move that fast before?" Eddie asked.

"Nope," I said, glancing back over my shoulder. "'Specially not on crutches."

"Didn't even use his legs," Eddie said, with a touch of awe. "Had those ol' crutches whippin' around like spokes on a wheel. Do you think he was ever an acrobat in a circus?"

"Probably."

1. What two examples of exaggeration can you find in this passage?

2. How does that exaggeration make the story more humorous?

    Now check your answers with your teacher. Review this lesson if you don't understand why an answer was incorrect.

WRITING ON YOUR OWN ①

In this exercise you will use what you learned in this lesson to write two or three paragraphs describing your humorous event. Follow these steps:

- Review the list of ideas and notes you wrote for Writing: Developing a Humorous Essay. Choose one of the events to describe. Before you write your description, think about what facts or details you will exaggerate. Look at McManus's essay again for ideas to help you add exaggeration to your description.
- Using your notes to help you, write two or three paragraphs describing the event. Include at least one example of exaggeration.
- When you have finished writing your paragraphs, reread them. Could you add other information that would help your reader get a clearer mental picture of the event? Does your exaggeration add to the humor of the event?

LESSON ②   DESCRIPTIVE LANGUAGE AND FORESHADOWING

Good descriptions are clear and vivid. They make a scene seem to come to life by focusing on details that help the reader to form a mental picture of what is happening. In "A Good Deed Goes Wrong," author McManus uses carefully chosen words to create vivid images. His use of descriptive language helps readers see Rancid flying down the run and hear his scream as he hits the funnel.

Read this passage from the essay, trying to visualize the scene. What words or phrases make the scene come to life?

> The skid trail had been gouged into the mountains by old-time loggers dragging logs down it. In fact, it was so steep they probably didn't have to drag the logs but merely had to roll them into it and let them shoot to the bottom of the mountain. Erosion had cut the trail down to bare rock, which was now coated with ice, making it even better for a toboggan run. When we were building up our curved bank to funnel the track into the skid trail, Eddie slipped and nearly shot down the run with nothing but his body, and would have if he hadn't managed to grab a small tree and pull himself back up.
>
> "Wow!" he said. "This is going to be good!"

McManus has created a visual image. Look at the words and phrases he uses to describe the skid trail: *gouged into the mountains; steep; shoot to the bottom; bare rock coated with ice;* and *shot down the run.* The author's choice of words helps readers to picture the steep, ice-coated rock skid trail and Eddie slipping and nearly shooting down the run.

Did you notice that the author makes a point of emphasizing how steep and slippery the skid trail is? He is suggesting that it could be dangerous to make a run down it. He reinforces this idea by describing how Eddie slips and saves himself from shooting down the run by grabbing a small tree. He tells you Eddie's reaction: "Wow! This is going to be good!" Whether you realize it or not, McManus is hinting at something that is going to happen later in the story. What do you think he is hinting at?

When an author provides a hint or clue about future events, he or she is using a technique called *foreshadowing.*

Foreshadowing helps to build suspense. The author wants readers to speculate, or guess, what will happen later. Whether you guess correctly or are completely surprised by what happens, the use of foreshadowing increases interest and reader involvement in the story.

EXERCISE ②

Read these two passages from the essay. Use what you have learned in this lesson to answer the questions that follow them.

"My gosh, it's a bobcat. Feel it. It must have just been killed. It's still warm. Look, it's got a bit of blood on its head where the car hit it, but otherwise it's in great shape". . . .

"Hey, wait a minute," I said. "I know what we'll do. We'll give it to Rancid."

Presently, Rancid stopped snoring. He muttered something in his sleep. Then he apparently banged the table with his arm, because we heard a bump and then the sound of the matchbox hitting the floor.

"Darn," Eddie whispered. "The matchbox fell out from under the bobcat's chin. The surprise is ruined now."

"Whazzat?" Rancid mumbled. "What in tarnation . . . ? GOL-DANG! GIT! GIT AWAY FROM MEEEE!"

Eddie and I chuckled.

The table crashed to the floor. A chair was flung against the wall and a block of firewood sailed out the door. All of this was accompanied by a terrible roaring and snarling and the wildest cussing I had ever heard.

"GIT BACK! GIT BACK!" Rancid yelled amid all the bangs and crashes and thumps.

Eddie looked at me. "I didn't think he'd be this sur-prised."

"No fooling," I said nervously. "Maybe we'd better leave right now. We can tell him later about our present for him, when he isn't so surprised."

At that moment there was a furious rattling of crutches and Rancid burst out of the cabin, shot across the yard and into his privy, slamming the door shut behind him.

1. What sentence in the first passage foreshadows what hap-pers later, in the second passage?

2. McManus's use of descriptive language in the second pas-sage creates vivid images. What words and phrases does he use to create images that appeal to the senses of sight and hearing?

Now check your answers with your teacher. Review this lesson if you don't understand why an answer was incorrect.

 WRITING ON YOUR OWN ②

In this exercise you will use what you learned in this lesson to add comic images and, perhaps, foreshadowing to your description. Follow these steps:

- Reread the paragraphs you wrote for Writing on Your Own 1. Think about what you have learned about how McManus uses descriptive words to create humorous images and how he uses foreshadowing.
- Underline the descriptive words that you have used in your paragraphs. Do you see places where you could add descriptive language to make your retelling of the event more humorous? For example, imagine that you described giving

your dog a bath this way: "When Rover jumped out of the tub, he knocked it over, splashing everything in sight." By adding descriptive language, you might improve your description this way: "When Rover leaped frantically out of the tub, he sent it crashing to the floor, engulfing me and Mother's freshly ironed white-trimmed red dress in a tidal wave of soapsuds and water."

• Now think of how you might add foreshadowing to your description. Using the same sample sentences about Rover, you could add this sentence to create foreshadowing: "Staring in disbelief at this scene of total disaster, I said to myself, 'Don't worry; I'll clean up this mess, and then I'll dry and iron Mom's dress again. She'll never know what happened.'"

• Now rewrite your description, using descriptive language to create a vivid picture for your readers. If possible, add fore-shadowing to your narration of the event.

• When you have finished rewriting your paragraphs, reread them. Does your language create a vivid image? Is the description humorous? Have you added foreshadowing?

LESSON 3   IRONY AND HUMOR

A major element of humor is irony. *Irony* is the contrast between what appears to be and what really is or between what is expected to happen and what actually happens. Verbal irony and understatement are two types of irony. McManus uses both types in his essay.

Verbal Irony *Verbal irony* is the contrast between what a writer or a character says and what he or she actually means. You probably hear examples of verbal irony every day. If you've gotten a particularly bad haircut and your friend says "Nice hair," he or she is using verbal irony. Look for the author's use of verbal irony in the following passages describing the sled run that the two boys have made.